ARTISTS IN
NAZI-OCCUPIED FRANCE:
A GERMAN OFFICER'S MEMOIR

ARTISTS IN NAZI-OCCUPIED FRANCE:

A GERMAN OFFICER'S MEMOIR

WERNER LANGE

TRANSLATED BY LEONARD ROSMARIN

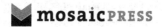

Library and Archives Canada Cataloguing in Publication

Lange, Werner, 1911-1980?
[Artistes en France sous l'Occupation. English]
    Artists in Nazi-occupied France : a German officer's memoir
/ Werner Lange.

Translation of: Les artistes en France sous l'Occupation.
Includes bibliographical references and index.
Issued in print and electronic formats.
ISBN 978-1-77161-330-9 (softcover).--ISBN 978-1-77161-330-9
(softcover).--ISBN 978-1-77161-331-6 (HTML).--ISBN 978-1-77161-332-3
(PDF).--ISBN 978-1-77161-374-3 (Kindle)

    1. Artists--France--History--20th century. 2. France--
Intellectual life--20th century. 3. France--History--German
occupation, 1940-1945--Personal narratives, German. I. Title.
II. Title: Artistes en France sous l'Occupation. English

N6848.L3613 2018   709.4409'044   C2018-903081-X
                                            C2018-903082-8

Published by MOSAIC PRESS, Publishers, Oakville, Ontario, Canada, 2019.
Copyright © 2015 Groupe Artège Éditions du Rocher - 28, rue Comte Félix Gastaldi - BP 521 - 98015 Monaco www.editionsdurocher.fr
Translation Copyright © 2019 Mosaic Press & Leonard Rosmarin

ONTARIO ARTS COUNCIL
CONSEIL DES ARTS DE L'ONTA
an Ontario government agency
un organisme du gouvernement de l'On
We acknowledge the Ontario Arts Council
for their support of our publishing program

We acknowledge the Ontario Media Development Corporation
for their support of our publishing program

Funded by the Government of Canada
Financé par le gouvernement du Canada | Canada

MOSAIC PRESS
1252 Speers Road, Units 1 & 2
Oakville, Ontario L6L 5N9
phone: (905) 825-2130

info@mosaic-press.com

TABLE OF CONTENTS

PREFACE

Werner Lange wrote these "memoirs" before hanging himself.

These are not classic war memoirs, nor are they even memoirs of the Paris Occupation in the way we imagine them. One does not find here either military activity, struggles against Resistant fighters, terrorist attacks, or persecution of Jews. The author is an intellectual, he is a subtle, cultivated Francophile. The people who file past us are arts personalities, painting and sculpture geniuses whose works take their places among the treasures of the great museums, and are found in the most prestigious collections. Their names appear in all the textbooks of art history. I will not quote them here, you will discover them in the following pages, and in positions that were not always flattering. Not because of any despicable conduct or criminal political activities, but because they tried to live normally when normality was out of the question, to even acquire wealth in some cases at a time when the Nazi occupier laid down the law.

Collaborators.[1] They were collaborators, if you wish, but also admirable artists! Collaborators who did not clamour for the massacre of Jews, or write books like *Les Décombres (The Debris)*,[2] or publish in *Je suis partout (I Am Everywhere)*,[3] collaborators who painted, sculpted, exhibited, had dealings with the occupier in order to continue painting, exhibiting, earning money, and, for some, eating better.

The interest of this text, indeed, its fascinating side, lies precisely in its frank, almost naive descriptions of everyday life. The war and the Occupation

---

1. The term, "Collabo" that appears in the original French text, and is the shortened version of the word "Collaborateur", carries with it a nuance of contempt. (Translator's note)

2. An influential book by Lucien Rebatet, a best-seller during the Occupation.

3. A newspaper in which Robert Brasillach published during the war his calls to murder.

are there, but evoked from the vantage point of the restrictions, troubles, difficulties in moving about and finding gasoline, the problems that artists faced in obtaining the colours they needed to paint or the metals they required to cast their sculptures.

Books have already been written about the artistic life in the Paris of that time. We know that it was rich, productive and fruitful. Great films were made between 1940 and 1944, masterpieces like *Les enfants du paradis* (*Children of Paradise*) by Marcel Carné or *Les Corbeaux* (*The Crows*) by Henri-Georges Clouzot. Jean Cocteau, Sacha Guitry, Jean-Paul Sartre filled theatre halls. Music, painting, opera: the artistic effervescence was evident in all the domains of art.

The captivating quality of these pages lies not in the description of events that people who are interested in this period of history know already, and that one can find in other works, but in the anecdotal, everyday, banal nature of the lives these celebrities led under the occupation. It is precisely this indecent, almost "people" aspect that makes the book so unique and interesting. The fact that these events were related by an officer of the *Propagandastaffel* (Propaganda Squadron), but a young man full of admiration for the artistic luminaries he had to deal with, whom he had to "take care of," gives the narrative an incomparable colour. The genuine friendship that linked Lange to Maillol or Vlaminck, his close relationships with Derain and others, gave rise to previously unpublished material of a richness that no history book can lay claim to.

After the end of the war, Werner Lange moved back to Paris as soon as it was possible, because he loved the arts and loved France. He continued frequenting the people he had known during the war. And if he committed suicide, it was not caused by issues connected to the time of the Occupation. It resulted from a love affair. In any event this is what they told me. These photos and this text written directly in French and which he never attempted to publish while he was alive, thus came naturally into the possession of his friend A.C., a well known figure of Parisian night life in the 70's and 80's and owner of gay establishments. To offset financial difficulties, he sold them to M.C., a renowned Russian painter and sculptor and well-informed collector living in France and the United States. A friend. So the "Dr. Lange" dossier lay dormant in one of his cupboards until October 2014. It was removed from that place following a conversation about Dina Vierny, herself a Russian émigré and a famous gallery owner as well as Maillol's inspiration, muse and heiress. And a character in this book.

So the text fell into my hands a bit like in the *Manuscit trouvé à Saragosse* (The Manuscript Found in Saragossa), [4] or in *Moravagine*. [5] On reading and re-reading these pages written in a French that had to be reworked without making it lose its colour and originality, I would catch myself saying "That can't be true!," so much was I under the impression of being in *Un Américain à Paris (An American in Paris)*, [6] or rather in an improbable *Un Allemand à Paris (A German in Paris)*. Because the *dandy* side of Lieutenant Lange, his friendly and even at times "schoolgirl" side, makes this narrative unique and engaging in a paradoxical way. It is unique through the "exclusive" nature, if I may call it, of the stories he tells, because the private episodes related here (there is practically nothing else) possess an intimate quality owing to the fact that Werner Lange was the only one present there. He alone accompanied Arno Breker on his solitary trip across France. He alone dined with Picasso in a black market clandestine brothel. He alone travelled to Banyuls to convince Maillol to come to Paris for the inauguration of the big Breker exhibit. He alone would spend Sundays at the Vlamincks and Utrillos. He alone received spontaneous gifts from French artists that were destined for Joseph Goebbels. He alone saved Dina Vierny almost by accident from the claws of the Gestapo.

The many previously unpublished episodes of this book thus stand out through their astonishingly private nature, their singular psychological veracity. It is as though one were living next to these great artists and gallery owners; as though one were strolling with them on the streets of an occupied but so lively Paris, a city that has not stopped fascinating us seventy years after the end of the war.

Dr. Lange's gift as a storyteller, the kindly sharpness of his gaze as a privileged witness, immersed in a fascinating milieu at a particularly dramatic time in French history, make this a captivating book that one reads as though one were watching a film.

Victor Loupan, Editor

---

4. A novel by Jean Potocki.

5. A novel by Blaise Cendrars.

6 . A musical comedy film by Vincent Minnelli.

FOREWORD

The Second World War has been over for decades now, and yet we continue talking about the war, the Occupation, and the France of Vichy. Time has passed, but these subjects are still on everyone's lips. Dozens of books, radio and television programs have been devoted to this period, as though it continued to fascinate, teach and nourish our consciousness.

This is what prompted me to immerse myself again in my notes which are certainly personal, but which evoke four dramatic years in the History of France, years described by the term "Occupation."

As a German, I was on the other side. I was an occupier. Thus I saw the period from a perspective that was different than yours. Even though I was an occupier, I was among those Germans who knew and loved French culture more than any other.

WL

MY MODEST LIFE

I was born in 1911, in Leipzig, a very beautiful cultural as well as commercial city, known long ago for its international fairs.

After the 1914-1918 war, my family settled in Kassel, in the state of Hesse, where my father, a company head, directed a metallurgical factory. So it was in that former capital of the kingdom of Westphalia, whose chateau is moreover well known in France, because Napoleon III was imprisoned there after the disaster of Sedan, that I spent my childhood and youth. There, too, I discovered, thanks largely to my father, my strong inclination for the arts. As a high school student, I pursued an artistic training program along with my regular studies in the studios of various artists in the Academy.

In 1931, with my first university diploma in my pocket, I would have wanted to launch my career as a painter, but my mother strongly insisted that I study the history of art. She was afraid, not without reason, that as an artist I would not always have enough to eat.

At the time, in Germany at any rate, when one wished to study the history of art, the choice of the professor under whose tutelage one wanted to learn, also determined the choice of the university. And since I wished to study under Professor Panofsky, who enjoyed a world-wide reputation, I found myself at the University of Hamburg. This was, I repeat, in 1931. Two years later, Hitler came to power and Professor Panofsky was obliged to leave Germany. He went to teach at Harvard University, where he was offered a chair. Sad and disoriented, I didn't know what to do. Professor Panofsky was, in my eyes, irreplaceable. But I simply had to continue my studies. So I decided to pursue them with Professor Pinder, at the University of Munich. His teaching was the very opposite of Professor Panofsky's. But the Bavarian capital still retained, in 1933, its libertarian and anti-authority spirit, its tradition and, at the same time, its artistic taste marked by the "Blaue Reiter" period. [1] In addition to my university studies, I painted a great deal, without taking into account the new regime's taste for doctrinarian realism which would soon become the official art of the Third Reich.

In 1935, when Professor Pinder was engaged by Humboldt University in Berlin, I followed him because I wanted to complete my thesis devoted to Notre-Dame of Dresden. This marvel would be totally destroyed by allied bombardments at the end of the war. So I followed him and became, as I hoped I would, a Doctor in Philosophy. In Germany at that time the history of art was taught in the faculty of philosophy.

Coming from a well-to-do family, I had, during the course of my studies, visited Italy which, since Goethe, greatly attracted young German romantics like myself. But it was France that I visited and loved the most. I can't tell you to what extent I was moved on discovering with my own eyes those marvellous cathedrals the plans of which I carried in my head. In Paris, I spent hours and days studying Notre Dame. But even more than the historical monuments, I was drawn to contemporary art. That's because all the great artists who lived in France enjoyed an extraordinary reputation beyond the Rhine.

Having succeeded brilliantly in my studies and in possession of my beautiful diploma, I joined the State Museum in Berlin. Unfortunately, the Nazi hurricane had already swept through there, and I could no longer find many paintings that I so loved, and artists that I had even known in Paris. They were henceforth classified in the category of "degenerate art." As a result, the "contemporary art" section of our museum had been emptied of a good portion of its masterpieces. Fortunately, Professor Justi, [2] who had assembled this important collection, was still there. With so many works removed, he had also lost his position as director and would not go to his office more than once a week. And even on that day, he did not have much to do. So we talked a great deal. Discretely, of course. I still keep, preciously, the memory of his "memories."

---

1. Blaue Reiter or Blue Horseman, a group of Munich artists with expressionistic tendencies, of which Vassili Kandinsky and Paul Klee were part. (Editor's Note, henceforth referred to by the abbreviation EdN)

2. Founder in 1919 of the Kronprinzenpalais Museum, the first German museum of modern art, Ludwig Justi was a major figure in European cultural life in the period between the wars. His museum would be closed in 1933. (EdN)

In 1939, I was working for the Union of the Museums of Berlin. And I remember very well that day of September 9, when the radio station of the little town of Gleiwitz, in Upper Silesia, was attacked by the Polish troupes. I didn't know, at the time, that they were really German soldiers in disguise. And that the Nazi government had manufactured this provocation for the purposes of attacking Poland.

It was war!

Once the hostilities began, our priorities changed. It was no longer possible to work normally. It became necessary to protect the art works, to evacuate them as a precautionary measure, to shelter them. The Nazi regime, which had nevertheless wanted and prepared the war, had not given the slightest thought to protecting the art works, masterpieces with which German museums were overflowing. How could one evacuate and where could one hide the Pergamon altar, the bust of Nefertiti, Rembrandt's *Golden Helmet*, or *Watteau's Enseigne de Gersaint*? (*The Sign of Gersaint*)

I learned later from Jacques Jaujard, the General Manager of the Louvre, that France, contrary to Germany, had indeed taken its precautions and knew when, where and how to remove its art masterpieces. One year before the beginning of the war, in 1938, a large part of the Louvre's collections had already left Paris. In his office, at the Louvre, during the Occupation, Jacques Jaujard would show me the long row of books and bound catalogues, in which all the movements of the art works were carefully noted. At the beginning of the war, all of the Louvre's halls were deserted. Only *l'Artémis de Versailles* (*The Artemis of Versailles*) had remained. Jaujard explained to me that the marble sculpture was too fragile to be transported by truck. He had thus made the risky decision to leave it where it was.

The same did not hold true for Berlin. So in September 1939, we engaged in feverish and doggedly determined activity in all the sections of the museum. It was insane. We had to unhook certain art works, remove others from their showcases, wrap them, have made-to-measure carts produced to transport them. And what to do with hundreds and thousands of precious books, certain of which were of priceless value? It was crazy! One day, when passing through the archeological section filled with Greek marbles, I came upon its director, Professor Wieckert. He was looking at a beautiful marble head that was going to be wrapped up and removed. It seemed as though he was viewing it for the first time. He didn't say anything, but one could tell from the expression on his face that he believed he would never see it again.

Obviously, the Pergamon altar could not be put in a crate. And to pull free the relief plaques would have taken an enormous amount of time. So we made the decision to protect this combat between gods and gipsies by surrounding it with sand bags. It was a bad decision, because the marbles became quite yellow on contact with the damps sand. Alas, I only noticed this after the war.

Since I had barely left the University, I had not received any military training. So I was left alone in my museum. But on February 13 1940—I remember this as though it happened yesterday--I received a notification, or rather the order to appear right away at a barracks, far from Berlin.

It was out of the question to disobey. So the next day, I arrived in Frankfort-on-the-Oder, with a valise under my arm. I was to learn to march in step, salute and become a gunner. The drill sergeant, who had never before encountered someone who worked in a museum, often asked me if one could really earn a living by plying such a "trade." After a few weeks of exercises, it was my education more than my skills as a draughtsman that opened up the doors to the office of the boss. And my life changed completely. Henceforth, I spent my time designing strategic plans, even participating in their elaboration. The battalion head, who had directed a large bank in Berlin before the war, quickly realized that, when all was said and done, this technical work corresponded neither to my training nor my temperament. He, thus, had me transferred to propaganda services. And thanks to this transfer I received not only the rank of officer, but found myself back in Paris the same year with a position

PARIS

In Paris, the *Propagandastaffel*, in other words, the German propaganda service, occupied a modern building at 52 avenue des Champs-Élysées.

Assigned to the cultural section, my direct boss was Lieutenant Lucht, a close collaborator of Joseph Goebbels, the Reich's Minister of Propaganda. Some people said that he was even a friend of Dr. Goebbels. Our section covered mainly three domains of activity: theatre, music and fine arts. I was in charge of fine arts and dealt principally with all that was "living art:" artists themselves (painters and sculptors), exhibits, galleries, salons and other artistic manifestations, big or small. The instructions were very clear: I had to spy on everybody and stick my nose everywhere. At that time, I already knew very well the cultural policy of the Nazi regime: it consisted in stifling any new action and in imposing the party line on artists. The fight against "degenerate art" had considerably drained the terrain inasmuch as everything that was not conformist was "degenerate" and, as such, was condemned to death. Barlach, Pechstein, Kokoschka were blacklisted. They no longer had the right to work, they could not exhibit and their works had been removed from museums. The Bauhaus, the cradle of modern art, had to close its doors, and the artists who used to teach there had to leave Germany. This happened to Klee, Kandinsky, Gropius and many others. Foreign artists didn't escape this either. Paintings by Matisse, Léger or Picasso were taken down and disappeared for good.

I knew all of that. And I did not approve it. But my military status demanded of me an attitude contrary to my convictions as well as to the true values of art. As I conceived them, in any event. I could not obey the orders of the *Propagandastaffel*; I was obliged to do so, however. It was necessary, then, for me to show humanity and adapt to the situations in order to avoid levelling reproaches against myself. All false modesty aside, I believe I succeeded in keeping both parties sweet, because my French friends never criticized me for anything, either during or after the war. I was able, moreover, to return to France after the war, to be reunited with my faithful friends, and to even settle there.

Paris during the Occupation was not the Paris I had loved so much before the war. The difficulties tied to the war and the restrictions under the German Occupation made everyday life painful: ration tickets, curfews, streets without city lights. Of course, the Parisians who had fled to escape the offensive of the German army had returned to the capital. Paris was bustling as usual, full of life and fun. Even if France remained cut in half, even if its government headed by Marshal Pétain was in Vichy, in the free zone, Paris remained, despite the Occupation, a real capital where everybody wanted to live. I was among the first. A black market had been set up quickly, and those people who had a bit of money didn't lack for anything. Restaurants served meals without tickets, even though they didn't have the right to do so. Bicycles had replaced taxis, and young girls still laughed when walking down the Champs-Élysées, with their hair flying in the wind. Then the period of the pedal taxi was not long in coming: men with muscular thighs criss-crossed the streets at a fast clip, pulling trailers that could transport two passengers. Many people found that amusing. And since it was not expensive, everybody profited from it.

More than ever, women wanted to be fashionable. Since stockings were outrageously expensive on the black market, they would paint their legs with a dye made with tea essence as its base, and even drew the seams with black lines on their calves. As there was simply no leather at all available on the market, shoes were fashioned with cloth, on wood soles. You can believe me, one would see very elegant shoes in the stores, the kind that would easily satisfy the most capricious of bourgeois ladies. The only flaw these shoes had was the noise they made at every step. Without being in the least embarrassed, the ladies made the best of a bad bargain, and the whole of France sang the refrain of Maurice Chevalier: "The wooden soles go click-clack." One could find everywhere the pre-war perfumes, particularly sought out by the German soldiers who would buy them for their wives and fiancées, often French ones. Chanel No. 5 was already the most famous of perfumes.

High fashion was also in full swing. The salons, vying in splendor with one another, were in constant competition: Maggy Rouff [1] reigned on the Champs-Élysées and Schiaparelli [2] at Place Vendôme; Lucien Lelong, Marcel Rochas, Germaine Lecomte [3] would put out new models continuously, sometimes in taffeta, sometimes in lace. I don't know how they did it, but despite the war and the hardships, the great Parisian high fashion designers always managed to obtain the necessary material. The milliners also created real marvels, mountains of ribbons and flowers. The Albouy salon, on rue du Colisée, set the tone for Parisian extravagances.

The theatre was thriving, too. At the Comédie française, *Le Soulier de Satin* (*The Satin Slipper*) by Paul Claudel played to full houses. On the boulevards, big audiences flocked to applaud Edwige Feuillère. The Théâtre de la Madeleine presented to sold-out houses Sacha Guitry's comedy *N'écoutez pas, Mesdames* (*Don't Listen, Ladies*), in which he triumphed in the main role. Despite her age, Cécile Sorel performed marvellously the role of Marie-Antoinette in the drama by Marcelle Marette *Madame Capet*, that played to sold-out houses at the Théâtre Montparnasse. As for Alice Cocéa, [4] she enchanted her audiences at the Théâtre des Ambassaderus, in Crommelynck's *Le Cocu magnifique* (*The Magnificent Cuckold*). In 1941, she would moreover take over the management of that theatre.

The cinemas were also drawing crowds. The young and handsome Jean Marais had instantly become a big star, thanks to Jean Cocteau's *L'Éternel retour* (*The Eternal Return*). Naturally, contrary to the theatre which remained very purely French, the cinema underwent the influence of the occupying power. Many German productions were projected in the halls. Often mediocre on the artistic level, the German films were used essentially as propaganda and the French movie goers stayed away from them, the Parisians in any event. Even the best known of German films of that period, *Le juif Süss* (*The Jew Süss*), hardly drew crowds.

Just as in the thirties, the important music-halls produced revues full of

---

1. Marguerite Besançon de Wagner, known as Maggy Rouff, and a fashion designer of Belgian and German origin. (EdN)

2. An Italian fashion designer, Elsa Schiaparelli is especially noted as the inventor of *Rose shocking*. (EdN)

3. French fashion designers. (EdN)

4. An actress, singer, stage director and theatre manager of Roumanian origin, whose big career came to an abrupt end at the Liberation. (EdN)

feathers, superficial gloss and flashy jewelry that so pleased working-class audiences. The Casino de Paris, the Folies Bergères, the Tabarin played to full houses every night. Yvette Guilbert, Maurice Chevalier, Cléo de Mérode[5] were more popular than ever. Mistinguett, who had slipped away for a moment, resurfaced after the armistice, and sang *Titine* every night in her hoarse voice as well as showed off her beautiful legs in her famous *Dance des Apaches* (Apache Dance). The Lido, a hall in the basement of the Claridge Hotel on the Champs-Élysées, was always full, too.

---

5. Céopâtre-Diane de Méode, otherwise known as Cléo de Mérode, was a dancer and an icon of French beauty. Contrary to what the author affirms, she withdrew to the area of the Indre during the Occupation. In 1950, Cléo de Mérode won a lawsuit against Simone de Beauvoir who compared her unfairly to a "cocotte" (a lady of loose morals) in *The Second Sex*. (EdN)

52 AVENUE DES CHAMPS-ÉLYSÉES

Obviously, I was far from living it up every day. I was there above all to work, and I worked conscientiously.

The seats in the corridor that led to my study were taken by storm as soon as the offices opened. In fact, this corridor served as a waiting room. Whether they had appointments or not, many people thronged there from the morning onwards. They were often pretty secretaries, sent by gallery owners who thought no doubt that I was susceptible to the charms of their young employees. Which was not the case. So they waited their turn patiently, their eyes riveted on the door, with a little piece of paper in their hand. On the paper were most often noted down the dates of the next exhibition because no preview could take place without my signature accompanied by a stamp. Even I cannot remember ever having refused to sign or stamp these little pieces of paper.

There were not just supplicants and beggars. That would have been too sad. There were also people who came to chat as good friends, or at least as good acquaintances. Painters and even their wives came to see me, just like that; to chat, to peddle gossip, stories of intrigue, accounts of enmities. After she returned to Paris and moved into the Hôtel Bristol, Cécile Sorel would often visit almost as a neighbour. Mistinguett came up too, but never "just like that," she always had a personal request deep in her handbag. Lucie Valore, Utrillo's wife, paid me frequent visits to talk to me interminably about her husband's paintings, and also, not so incidentally, about her own. Odette Patridès' Gallery had the exclusive rights to Utrillo's works. She exhibited permanently his recent works, because his paintings of Montmartre enjoyed great success; she also published his monographs and so needed my *Imprimatur* each time. Just like Louis Carré who organized an exhibition of the drawings and pastels of

Maillol and published, for that occasion, an album containing all the works displayed. An Album for which Maurice Denis and Pierre du Colombier wrote the preface.

But it was unquestionably at the Charpentier Gallery that the most important art events were produced. The Gallery occupied a private mansion, opposite the Élysée Palace, on rue du Faubourg Saint-Honoré. On the ground floor, a beautiful vestibule led to an immense hall bedecked in red velvet. By climbing a few steps of an elegant little incline, one reached several exhibition halls. Over to the right, a large staircase led to the salons of the first floor, more intimate than those below. The administration and the secretariat were also on the first. There sat enthroned Raymond Nacenta, assisted by his faithful secretary, Mademoiselle Rollando. This veritable enterprise was not just a gallery, but also a publishing house for art books, and the editorial offices of the review Collection Comoedia-Charpentier, which devoted special editions to famous names like Arthur Honegger, Maillol, and others. The exhibitions, always well conceived and carefully executed, were at times dedicated to the works of a great painter, van Dongen for example, or to a theme: hunting, a century of watercolours, etc. The activity of the Charpentier Gallery was not only of a commercial nature. Based on the gallery's important watercolour collection, the art historian and professor at the Sorbonne Louis Réau published, for example, an important academic work of erudition which, quite obviously, could not be a money-maker. Despite the war and the Occupation, the previews at the Charpentier Gallery were social events of the first water, where an elegant crowd flocked, as much to see the works exhibited as to be seen.

The person I would liaise with at Charpentier's was the Count de Laborde, the assistant in the business, a man of rare elegance, a true lord of former times. The Count had travelled a great deal before the war, and liked to tell me about his trips, especially the ones he made in Pomerania, in Potsdam where with his father he had visited the magnificent chateau of Sans-Souci built by Frederick-the-Great. This is a magical place if there ever was one, full of memories of Voltaire's sojourns. One day, when they were crossing the park in the direction of the New Palace, behind which stood a little railway station to facilitate the arrivals of the imperial family, they noticed an extraordinary ballet. Guards were active on the quay as a little train arrived from which three personages came down: a very elderly bearded man, and two other people, one of whom was very young. These were indeed the three Emperors of Germany: Wilhelm I, Frederick and Wilhelm II; the father, the son and the grandson. This was in 1888, a year which remained inscribed in German history as the "year of the three emperors!" And the young Count de Laborde had seen them! This was one of the stories he liked to tell the most.

THE GERMANS

As early as 1940, the occupying German army was followed by an army of civilians, of profiteers of all kinds.

It must be said that many Germans lived in Paris before 1939. At the beginning of the war, they were forced to leave France, to abandon their residences. They returned, then, after the armistice, which was, let us say, normal. But these former residents, who were really returning to their homes, were followed by a crowd of disreputable people, guided by their little opportunistic noses, who decided to try their luck in Paris. One should know that there were at the time in the capital many empty and, indeed, quite simply abandoned apartments. They were abandoned because their owners were Jewish, or because those who used to live there had preferred to take refuge in the free zone. These cozy, entirely furnished nests, often located in the elegant neighbourhoods, were quickly snapped up by these unscrupulous profiteers who got rich quickly thanks to the black market. On the surface, Paris lacked everything. But on the surface only. Because one could also find everything by paying the required price. There was no lack of customers. On the one hand, there remained fortunate French citizens, and on the other, there were greedy and immoral Germans. Obliged, in principle, to repress the black market, the latter were its most faithful customers. So the "market" expanded by the minute. And the traffickers would pile up their gold ingots as though they were match boxes. It was enormous! Moreover, the most wily of the fraudsters did not limit themselves to France; they had entire freight trains going to Germany. Understanding its advantage, Germany would swiftly create a "legal" service for the purchase of illegal merchandise. State agents, provided with the appropriate papers, criss-crossed France specially for that. All domains were concerned, including the fine arts.

Hitler wanted to construct an immense museum in Linz, his native city, in Austria. And Professor Voss, the director of the important Dresden Gallery, was appointed director of this ambitious project, even though the construction of the building had not yet begun. In addition to overseeing the work per se, Professor Voss was given the task of bringing together all the art earmarked for the future museum's permanent collection. Missionaries with full pockets were sent to the four corners of occupied Europe. These were not brutes, but quite refined people, connoisseurs and art lovers. This is how Böhmer von Güstrow and Doctor Gurtitt, son of the celebrated art historian, arrived in Paris.

The reopening of the German embassy in Paris was, certainly, an event, but also an aberration. France had signed an armistice and not a peace treaty. The army thus controlled the conquered territory, and the military government, headed by General von Stülpnagel, administered occupied France. The setting up of a civil authority such as an embassy could only create tensions between the two powers. I cannot speak about everything, but in my particular domain, I can say that the treasures of the Louvre touched off a veritable war between the Embassy and the Hôtel Majestic, which was the headquarters of the military command in Paris. [1]

As I have already mentioned, even before France was invaded, the masterpieces of the Louvre had been evacuated and sheltered in the chateaux of Chambord, Valençay and Montal. With the arrival of the German troupes, these goods were placed under the protection of the army which had pasted small public notices with the following words: "This building, considered a historical monument, is placed under military protection." The commission for the protection of artworks in France, presided by Count von Metternich, was moreover part of the military administration. This service was responsible for the protection of the collections assembled from French museums, the Louvre being the first.

Otto Abetz, the new ambassador, and his wife Susanne, a Frenchwoman,

---

1. The Kommandantur. (EdN)

had taken possession of the splendid Hôtel Beauharnais, on the rue de Lille. [2] It was to a large extent thanks to this wife who had at one time been the secretary of Luchaire [3], the founder of *Nouveaux Temps* (New Times) [4], that Abetz would acquire an indisputable importance and achieve an acknowledged success.

In his capacity as ambassador, Abetz had asked the army to ensure that the Louvre's collections be returned to Paris. This request was not disinterested. The ambassador wanted to use these treasures as bargaining chips, with a view to future peace negotiations. But Count von Metternich refused outright. It was out of the question for him to touch the Louvre's goods, placed under the protection of the Commission for the Protection of Artworks, of which he was the president. Abetz was dumbfounded by the Count's reply. But Jacques Jaujard, the director of the Louvre, a man whom I knew well, was, on the contrary, very pleased. Metternich was a real lord, and a man of irreproachable integrity. So no one laid a finger on the artworks and they survived the war without harm.

The *Propagandastaffel* was under the jurisdiction of the military administration which was located, as I have already said, in the old building of the Hôtel Majestic, very close to the Étoile, on avenue Kléber. [5] Fortunately, I didn't have to betake myself to this former palace and I would go there only once a year. And just to the office for the distribution of coal, before the beginning of the cold season. The managers of this thankless service would come and go, and every year I would find myself facing a new head, obliged once again to go through the same farce as the previous year. Taking a long list with me, I

---

2. Built in 1714, this private mansion was acquired in 1803 by Prince Eugène de Beauharnais who made important transformations there, in the Empire style. The King of Prussia bought the building after the fall of the Empire and set up the royal legation there, which became the imperial embassy in 1871, then the embassy of the Weimar Republic in 1918, then that of Nazi Germany in 1933. It was in this dwelling that a cleaning woman, while rummaging in the wastepaper baskets, discovered the famous letter that launched the Dreyfus Affair. (EdN)

3. Jean Luchaire, journalist and newspaper owner, executed in 1946 at the fort of Chatillon. (EdN)

4. A highly influential collaboration newspaper. (EdN)

5. After having housed the German military High Command under the Occupation, the former Hôtel Majestic accommodated the seat of UNESCO, then services of the Ministry of Foreign Affairs, notably the Centre for International Conferences, before being sold by the French Government for 460 million Euros to The Public Investment Company of Qatar, Qatari Diat, which transformed it into a luxury hotel. At this address were signed the Paris Agreement that put an end to the Viet Nam War in 1973, the Paris Agreement on Cambodia in 1991 and the Kléber Agreement signed in 2003 after the northern rebellion in the Ivory Coast. (EdN)

would ask for tons of coal for my painters. Each time my requests were met by refusals, justified by the fact that Germans living in Paris would be given priority for coal. I would patiently explain to the new manager, as I had to the former one the year before, that painters were also human beings, and that they feared the cold. My arguments could be resumed in this way: "It is much colder in large studios than in apartments. And put yourself in the shoes of models who must pose in the nude in freezing temperatures. So go look into your stocks and deliver what I'm asking you."

Naturally, my arguments were longer than these few lines, but I always got what I wanted and left the Majestic with a smile on my face and coal vouchers in my pocket.

I frequented more often the Pass Service, on rue Galilée. For the obvious and simple reason that authorizations were necessary to cross the line of demarcation and enter the Free Zone. And to return, of course. In actual fact, I should not have gone there. Normally, pass seekers were supposed to come to my office, get a favourable note, then, armed with it, go to the rue Galilée. That was the procedure. Except that the bureaucrats in question would receive the requests, then let them gather dust in a drawer. Sometimes they would quite simply forget about them. To accelerate the procedure, I would gather the requests, and when I had a sufficient number, I would go in person to the rue Galilée. This way, I would have the famous Ausweis [6] within five minutes.

During the whole length of my stay in Paris, I did everything I could not to behave like an occupier. I did not frequent "the German colony" and had very little contact with Germans outside of my work. I especially avoided the crowd at the embassy. In the evenings I would go out; I had many friends, including the boxer Carpentier. [7] We would often meet at Léon Volterra's place, another friend who owned the Lido. Rudier [8] would also come often and pick me up at my office, then take me out with his friends to the country, in Robinson. Almost every Sunday I would go to Le Vésinet.

From the very beginning, I had asked for and received the authorization to dress as a civilian, even though, at least formally, I was an officer and so

---

6. The German pass, a precious document under the Occupation. (EdN)

7. Georges Carpentier, the glory of the boxing world, the first French world champion, a title he won in the United States in 1920. (EdN)

8. Eugène Rudier, son of Alexis Rudier, famous French foundry owners who produced the bronzes of the greatest sculptors of the time, including Rodin. (EdN)

obliged to wear the uniform. Obviously, my request contradicted military orders, especially in time of war, but I had explained to my superiors that the German uniform would complicate, and indeed compromise, my relationships with French artists. I was not wrong, because some of them became real friends. And I doubt whether this would have been possible if I had appeared at their homes in a German uniform.

The *de facto* distance I kept from the German authorities did not, however, have only advantages. I would be deprived of information as a matter of course. Being often absent, I did not know anything about what was being plotted at the Jeu de Paume Museum. I found out only after the war about this organized robbery of artworks that had belonged to Jewish collectors. [9]

---

9. Werner Lange is referring here to the pillaging of modern artworks, called "degenerate art" by the Nazis. Paintings by Picasso, Matisse, Van Gogh, owned by Jewish families, were stocked at the Jeu de Paume The most important works were stored in the Hall of the Martyrs. The Nazis would scatter these works, sell them or exchange them for paintings that were more to their taste. The French authorities took part in this shameful, but lucrative business, as much as did French art dealers and foreigners. (EdN)

TERECHKOVITCH

Kostia Terechkovitch [1] had come to obtain my agreement for the organizing of an exhibition at Petridès', on avenue Delcassé. I had already seen
certain paintings of his in any event. But I met him for the first time.

Kostia was an extremely likeable man. He had been born in 1902 in Moscow, where his father was a psychiatrist. But his inclination for the arts came
to him rather from his grandfather, an architect and friend of Chtchoukine,[2] a
great collector who had assembled in his personal gallery a quantity of very
important masterpieces that he bought when no one else wanted them. His
taste and his esthetic boldness had perhaps made him the most important modern art collector in Europe. Young Kostia could thus admire to his heart's content the works of Gauguin, Cézanne and Matisse. One day, Chtchoukine told
him that the richness of his artworks was not superficial, but that "everything
took place inside." This revelation determined his future.

A young prodigy, Kostia was admitted into the Fine Arts Academy when
he was only fifteen years old. But academic studies hardly interested him.
And then, there was the revolution in 1917. Blood and chaos. He had only one
idea at that time, to get to France, "the country of painters" where "everything
took place in the interior." After three years of wandering that took him to
the Ukraine, the Caucasus, Persia and Constantinople, Kostia finally reached

---

1. A French painter of Russian origin, Constantin Terechkovitch enlisted in the Foreign Legion
in 1939, to fight the Germans, but was demobilized after the defeat in 1940. Decorated with the
Legion of Honour in 1951, he died in Monaco in 1978. (EdN)

2. A buisinessman and great art collector, Serguei Chtchoukine would see his collection confiscated on the order of Lenin, in 1918. It forms the basis of the collection of western modern art
at the Hermitage and the Pushkin Museum in Moscow. He died in Paris in 1936. (EdN)

Paris, in 1920. He was eighteen. In Paris, cubism, sad and depressing, still reigned, whereas for Kostia, the city represented joie de vivre the "spring of life." I noted this phrase that Kostia had shared with me, and that he claimed came from Renoir, whom he admired enormously: "There are already so many annoying things in life, let's try not to manufacture more."

For this exhibition, Petridès had chosen from Kostia's studio a lively and harmonious ensemble, canvases covered with little touches so vivid, that one could only feel pleasure when looking at them. Female dancers from the Bal Tabarin were placed side by side with portraits of Matisse, Derain, Utrillo and Bonnard, other famous friends that Kostia had. Kostia was visibly happy to be a Parisian painter. It was the fulfillment of his fondest dream.

Obviously, I gave my approval for the setting up of this beautiful exhibition. To thank me, Kostia came back to see me with a work he dedicated to me: "To Doctor Lange, with my thanks to the nicest occupier I have ever met." That was in October 1942.

Three years later, in 1945, once the war was over, I found myself in the family country home, near Dresden. I was painting, while waiting for the disastrous and inhuman situation, resulting from the complete failure of Nazism, to stabilize. I had returned home shortly before when I received the order from the new communist municipal council to appear at the Russian "Komedatura" of the district. Not having harmed anyone, I wasn't too worried. I was wrong, because this visit, that I considered harmless, was going to be long and painful, in conformity with Russian practices, of the Soviet kind at least. Guided by some lucky star, I had taken a book from my library before starting my 15 kilometre trek on foot. And it was the very book Kostia Terechkovitch had offered me. As soon as I arrived, they threw me into a cell where I spent five long and painful days. After the fifth day, I was taken at midnight and led to the local commandant of the GPU. [3] All of my belongings were spread out on his desk, with Kostia's book well in the foreground. Uncomfortably seated on a stiff wooden chair, I underwent three hours of intense questioning, on my sojourn in Paris, my work during the Occupation, and... on Constantin Terechkovitch's dedication. Finally, his dry "Go back home!" put an end to this dangerous exercise. I was certain that I owed this unexpected denouement to Kostia's dedication. There was no other explanation for it. Because I had been summoned as a result of a slanderous denunciation, certainly concocted by the

---

3. Soviet secret services and repression, the ancestors of the KGB. (EdN)

new communist masters of our part of Germany. Moreover, they were very disappointed to see me come back home safe and sound.

A month earlier, a card from the Nice Casino had saved me from a prison camp on the Russian plains,[4] and this time Kostia's dedication saved me from death in a concentration camp in Siberia.

4. This episode is related in an subsequent chapter. (EdN)

THE SALONS

I had studied the history of art, so I understood the importance of the salons. I knew that David and Gros had acquired their reputations there. I also knew the story of Mademoiselle Victorine and *Le Déjeuner sur l'herbe* (The Luncheon On The Grass), rejected by the official Salon under Napoleon III, and which forced Manet to found, with other young artists, the famous Salon of The Rejected. I also knew the drawing that this story had inspired Manet to create: in it one could see gentlemen in top hats, walking with their paintings under their arms. The drawing was called *Messieurs les refusés!* (The Rejected Gentlemen).

I also knew about the history of the Salon d'automne (The Autumn Salon), where Georges Rouault presented his works for the first time. And where in 1905 erupted the scandal of the *Cage aux Fauves* (the Cage of the Wild Animals). It was the hall which exhibited the works of Vlaminck, Derain, Matisse, Friesz and Rouault, whose brutal colours shocked the "connoisseurs." And which, moreover, gave birth to fauvism.

Thus, I understood the danger of banning, which, more often than not, exposed one to ridicule.

Under the German Occupation, artist societies continued to function, almost as before. They would always organize their showings. More than at the Grand Palais, these would take place mainly at the Museum of Modern Art, built in 1937, for the World Fair. Also called the Palais de Tokyo, it was a vast building, stretching from the quays of the Seine till the avenue du Président Wilson.

The Society of French Artists and the National Society of Fine Arts had opened "Le Salon" (The Salon) there, an academic and perfectly boring event.

35

The Salon des Tuileries (The Tuileries Salon) was much more modern and more interesting. But the Salon d'automne always remained the most important. In short, things were still happening. For example, The Salon of Women Painters celebrated its 60 years in March 1944, with very beautiful retrospectives of Berthe Morisot, Suzanne Valadon and Marie Cassatt.

The truth of the matter is that these societies remained very free under the Occupation. As far as I was concerned, they would inform me simply of their preparations, and I would pay them a purely formal "monitoring visit." I was obliged, by my function, to give my green light as much for the artists as for the subjects exhibited, and I never banned or even asked about anything at all.

For example, in 1943, when I was inspecting the Autumn Salon, I found myself in a large hall, reserved for the works of George Braque... That was very courageous on the part of the organizers! In Germany, Braque was placed at the top of the list of "degenerate arts:" he was the *bête noire*. Nevertheless, this hall didn't frighten me, quite the contrary. I thought it was fortunate that so many of Braque's painting could be assembled in one spot. A landscape composed entirely of cubes drew my attention particularly. It was a small canvas. I found out later that from that painting emerged the term "cubism." Of course, I wondered how Berlin would react. And then I said to myself that there were a thousand kilometres between Paris and Berlin, and I decide to say nothing, and to let things proceed.

The salons were administered by Louis Hautecoeur, a State Councillor. It was up to him, in his capacity as a representative of the French State, to inaugurate them. This outdated formality already made me smile at that time. When I arrived at the Museum of Modern Art, I found M. Hautecoeur, a bit consternated I must say, who was waiting for me on the steps of the staircase, surrounded by... The Republican Guard! So we had to walk between the horses' tails to reach the portals, followed by a considerable crowd. Needless to say, I had never asked for, nor wished, to have this pomp. I must confess that these French formalities surprised me on more than one occasion.

THE SCHOOL OF FINE ARTS

I loved the Left Bank, the neighbourhood of galleries where the École des Beaux-Arts (The School of Fine Arts) was located. But the building itself hardly pleased me. Except for the right side of the main courtyard where one can still see the façade of Diane de Poitiers' Château d'Anet.

Whereas Paris was the world capital of modern art, the School of Fine Arts dispensed an official, very academic kind of teaching that lead to the Prix de Rome and a one-year stay at the Villa Médicis. Even though I'm rather indifferent to academism, I must confess that the School taught the craft well. It gave students good habits, without casting them into a mold on the artistic level. Maillol, Roussel and Vuillard passed through the School of Fine Arts in Paris, even if they later explored other options elsewhere. For example, in Gustave Moreau's studio.

It was Paul Landowski who administered the School of Fine Arts during the Occupation. One day, he kindly took me to see the so-called gallery of the "Prix de Rome," which exhibited good canvases with well-chosen subjects, but nothing more. Canvases that illustrated perfectly the "official" spirit of the school and its director.

Landowski was the sculptor who had decked out the Place de la Porte de Saint Cloud with fountains ten metres high, adorned at the base with bas-reliefs representing Paris and the Seine River. For some rather incomprehensible reason, these bas-reliefs were similar to Bacchanalian subjects of ancient Greece! Fortunately, the water that followed in front of them hid all that.

THE OPÉRA

The Opéra regained its place in Parisian artistic life as soon as the hostilities ended. One must say that this sumptuous edifice was clamouring for activity. I knew that before landing in the Palais Garnier, built under Napoléon III, the French Opéra, founded under Louis XIV, had occupied no less than twelve different halls. Even if the construction of this splendid building was completed under the Third Republic, this work by the architect Garnier remains a tribute to Napoléon III and, above all, to the Empress Eugénie.

Jacques Rouché [1] who ran the Opéra during the Occupation, had succeeded in creating, around Germaine Lubin [2] and José Beckmans, [3] a company of the highest order. As for the ballet, directed by Serge Lifar, a former principal dancer of Serge Diaghilev's Ballets Russes, it was quite simply the best in Europe.

Given the Occupation, Jacques Rouché had to present concerts of German music in the large hall of the Opera. And, in truth, that did not displease him! A great admirer of Wagner, he brought in the Berlin Opera with a *Tristan and*

1. An essential actor in French cultural life for a half-century, director of the Paris Opéra for more than thirty years, Jacques Rouché would be hauled before the civic chamber after the Liberation and relieved of his duties at the Opéra in 1945. (EdN)

2. A world-renowned French soprano, arrested and judged at the Liberation, Germaine Lubin was convicted of national indignity for life, denied access to certain places, and had her wealth confiscated. After the war, she devoted herself mostly to teaching and training. Régine Crespin, another opera luminary, was one of her students. (EdN)

3. A Belgian baritone with an international reputation, and a pillar of the Paris Opéra when Jacques Rouché was the director. (EdN)

Isolde that has remained forever in people's memories. [4] To the admirable Bayreuth cast, he added Germaine Lubin, an admirable, unforgettable Isolde. Placed under the direction of the young Berlin conductor Herbert von Karajan, the orchestra reached a level that none other could equal at that time in France.

Oddly enough, the performance of *Palestrina*, [5] an austere work and difficult to access by Hans Pfitzner, was also a triumph. A dazzling José Beckmans displayed gripping energy. Pfitzner, known for his fussy character, had made the trip to Paris specially to oversee the singers as much as the interpretation of his music. All this was very astonishing.

The young composer Werner Egk, [6] one of the most significant representatives of the new musical generation in Germany, also came to Paris to present his opera *Peer Gynt* that had already been performed triumphantly in many European capitals. His ballet *Joan von Zarissa*, choreographed and danced by Serge Lifar, was also received with a great deal of enthusiasm.

Thanks to the generous friendship of Jacques Rouché who had placed at my disposal a little box with direct access to the wings, which allowed me to go and greet my friends during the intermission, I was able to attend numerous performances. Since I was very close not only to Serge Lifar and Germaine Lubin, but to Serge Peretti, a principal dancer, I really went there very often.

When the Maillols sojourned in Paris, on the occasion of the exhibition by Breker, [7] I had tried to convince Mme Maillol, who liked opera very much, to accompany me. But they didn't have a car, and so could not travel easily from Marly to Paris. We remedied the situation during their next stay, because that time they were lodged at the Claridge, on the Champs-Élysées. [8] One Wednesday evening, a day for ballets, I enabled the Maillols to take advantage of my box. Lifar and Peretti were dancing Ravel's *Boléro*. During the intermission, I

---

4. In 1941, there was a performance by the Berlin Staatsoper given to celebrate the fall of Paris. Directed by Herbert von Karajan who was appointed by Hitler, it took place in the presence of Winifred Wagner, the general manager of the Bayreuth Festival, the daughter-in-law of Richard Wagner and a personal friend of Adolph Hitler. (EdN)

5. Created in Munich in 1917 by Bruno Walter, a Wagnerian work and a tribute to the masters of polyphony in the Renaissance. Pfitzner saw in Palestrina a manifesto against the new music embodied by Schönberg. (EdN)

6. A student of Carl Orff, Werner Egk committed his talent to the service of the "new music" demanded by the Third Reich. (EdN)

7. 1942. (EdN)

8. 1943. (EdN)

knew that it would give them pleasure to greet Lifar in his dressing room. He received us with his naked torso, a muscular, Cossack-like torso, full of grace, and very beautiful. Impressed, his eyes riveted on the dancer, Maillol asked him right on the spot to pose for a series of drawings. Obviously, Lifar accepted. And not only did he accept, but he also came to the Claridge every day the following week, for interminable posing sessions.

JEAN-GABRIEL DOMERGUE

Well before the war, during my sojourns in Paris, I had noticed paintings that adorned the windows of luxury shops, paintings that could not be missed. Sometimes they were bouquets of flowers, sometimes women with plunging necklines seated in theatre boxes, sometimes there were particularly lascivious nudes.

This really very prolific painter who supplied those shops was called Jean-Gabriel Domergue,[1] a very well-groomed--perhaps a bit too much so— bearded man. Despite not having talent or artistic taste, he had managed to get himself admitted into the society of well-to-do people, to such an extent that every large bourgeois apartment, although already overloaded, displayed his bouquets of flowers and portraits of "Madame at the theatre." Commissions came flooding in to the point where Domergue was becoming richer than his rich clients. He had a luxury apartment on the avenue d'Iéna, a dream property on the Côte d'Azur [2] and God knows how many others.

When I arrived in Paris, I quickly realized that Domergue's works were strangely absent from the luxury shops. I soon found out why, thanks to the extremely courteous visit from one of his lawyers, who explained everything. "His client" had not gone out of fashion, far from it. But "his client" had published caricatures of the "German government." Without seeing them, because his lawyer had not brought them to me, I understood that these were

---

1. A fashionable artist, especially prolific, Jean-Baptiste Domergue claimed to have invented the pin-up. A member of the Institut, an author of the very first poster of the first Cannes International Film Festival, he was for a time the curator of the Jacquemart-André Museum. (EdN)

2. Jean-Baptiste Domergue's house in Cannes was called "Villa Domergue" and was placed on the list of Historical Monuments. (EdN)

caricatures of Hitler. I was really very surprised. To tell you the truth, I could not imagine that a man painting such pictures could have political opinions. Obviously, he did. As a precautionary measure, he had retired to the Côte as soon as the German troops arrived. His cautiousness was justified, because his Paris apartment was sequestered.

"He is an artist, he should be forgiven," his lawyer told me. I followed him to Domergue's apartment. Immense! I had never see any as large: innumerable rooms succeeded one another, with rows of paintings on the wall. The main salon overlooking the avenue was transformed into a studio. On the easel was a large unfinished poster of Mistinguett, for a show at the Casino de Paris, postponed because of the arrival of the German troups.

Without having seen those famous caricatures, I thought that Domergue's offense could not be all that dreadful, and so I signed the paper allowing for his exoneration or his rehabilitation, as one wishes.

How many reproaches did I not endure as a result of this signature. Especially coming from merchants who could see Domergue again polluting the market. Sometimes they came up to me just to tell me: "Domergue is shit!"

That was true. But it was necessary to help him. And I could do so without harming myself. That is why I had signed the famous paper.

A nasty but funny story made the rounds about Jean-Gabriel Domergue:

"A painter dies and appears before Saint Peter who, when he learns that the former has painted naked women and done so in Paris, that modern Sodom and Gomorra, tells him:

"There is no place for you in Heaven!

The painter answers him:

"Since I have come so far, let me at least glance at it, to see what it is like."

Saint Peter opens the great portal a bit, and the dead painter sees angels on clouds, everything is very beautiful, except that he sees a man in the process of painting with a palette in his hand.

"But he's a painter! Why him and not me?"

"Not at all," replies Saint Peter, "he is not a painter, he is Jean-Gabriel!"

THE SAUCKEL MANEUVER

The unexpected appointment of Fritz Sauckel [1] at the head of the General Workforce Commission in France was a revolution in itself. [2] Placed under Hitler's direct orders, this former seaman, a Nazi from the very beginning, acquired so much importance that nobody would have dared meddle in his affairs. Narrow-minded and brutal, the man was frightening. The recruitment offices he had opened in Paris and the whole of France were separated from the military administration. Directed by subaltern civil servants who were incapable of taking initiatives but were good at carrying out orders, these offices functioned somewhat like a state within the state.

That is why when I saw Jean de Ruaz arriving at my place one day, looking half-dead, with a summons in his hand, I said to myself that I would not be able to help him. Two days later, he was supposed to show up at the Gare de l'Est, to join a convoy of workers leaving for Germany.

Ruaz ran a beautiful gallery on 31 avenue de Friedland. And he had two dependents: an already aged mother plus a young sister. Without him, the poor women would literally die of hunger. I knew that he was telling the truth. So I took up my pen to write a very firm letter and in German, a letter destined to impress the subaltern employees who were going to read it. I explained in it that M. Ruaz was a precious collaborator for me, indeed indispensable, and that he could not under any circumstances leave for Germany. On purpose, I signed very legibly: Dr. Lange.

---

1. An important Nazi dignitary, Fritz Stauckel was nicknamed "the slave-trader of Europe," because he was the one who organized the deportation of workers from occupied countries to Germany. (EdN)

2. 1942. (EdN)

I gave it to Ruaz for him to take to the office which had delivered the summons to him. One hour later, he returned, with a smile on his face.

Having succeeded in saving Ruaz from the claws of Sauckel's department, I discretely advised my little circle, my French friends, those close to me, to let me know as soon as they received a summons. I managed to save a number of others.

After the war, Ruaz and I remained in touch. He knew that I wished to return to France, as a friend. He tried to help me as best he could. That is how one day I received a document countersigned by police headquarters, in which Ruaz committed himself to assuming my travel and living expenses in France. In that period, it was *the* document that allowed me to cross the border.

WILDENSTEIN

Georges Wildenstein [1] was considered one of the great art dealers in the world. Obviously, seeing the turn of events, he had left his magnificent apartment on 57 rue La Boétie, and sought refuge in New York where he also ran a gallery bearing his name. His Parisian house had remained under the protection of one of his "Aryan" friends, a certain Monsieur Decoy.

I can't remember how I found out one day that some very fishy things were happening on the rue La Boétie. So I betook myself there, to get to the bottom of it. After all, according to my function, I had to keep abreast of everything that related to the arts, the galleries and the dealers.

Without being asked, M. Decoy informed me that he had received the visit of military and civilian Germans who, according to him, had come from Berlin. At the head of the group was a young woman! Decoy was absolutely sure: "She was the head." He told me that those people walked around the property, talked about the renovations and transformations to be undertaken. "They were carrying on like buyers," said M. Decoy. Intrigued, but above all rather rattled, I returned to the office to pass on the news to Lieutenant Lucht, my superior. Not only was Lucht not surprised, he told me he was the reason for this secret visit. More and more astonished, I discovered that he had received the order from Berlin to confiscate the Wildenstein gallery and replace it with a German one, to be managed by the young woman in question. Right then and there, I exploded in anger, in a way, moreover, that neither my grade nor my rank would have authorized.

"I'm the one who takes care of fine arts," I cried out in a rage! "No one else can touch it. And, especially, not the Wildenstein gallery!"

---

1. A gallery owner, collector, editor and historian of French art (1892-1963). (EdN)

I left slamming the door.

When I returned to my office, I realized that I had overstepped the limits. This was serious. This was the kind of action that could have me shipped to the Eastern front. Then, while thinking about it more and more, I reached the conclusion that there would not be any consequences. Without considering myself as irreplaceable, I was not easy to replace. Because the artists I took care of had become friends. Whoever would want to replace me would lose a lot of time trying to gain the confidence of the French artists. In addition, since my military papers had been misplaced, I was only a representative of the propaganda department. Lucht understood perfectly that my situation was atypical. On several occasions, he would have wished to decorate me, but could not do it. I could not be decorated for lack of military papers.

My reasoning had proven itself to be right. Because, not only was I not punished, but no one brought up the Wildenstein affair again. Except for Georges Wildenstein himself, when we had a very agreeable meeting after the war.

DAVID

I was sleeping peacefully in my room at the Hôtel Lincoln, when some hard knocking at the door woke me up suddenly. It was after midnight. I went to open it, rather worried, and found myself face to face with Emmanuel David,[1] shaking like a leaf.

I liked his gallery, on 52 rue du Faubourg Saint-Honoré. I had often spent some lovely moments there. The Drouant-David Gallery[2] was, moreover, known and respected in Paris. The exhibition rooms were located in the home of Helena Rubinstein, the lady of the beauty products. At the far end of one of the halls, there was a ping-pong table, on which we had often played.

That very evening, while he was at home, reading quietly, David heard some noise in front of its main entrance. When he went over, he found himself face to face with two Germans in uniform, who shouted at him: "Du Jude!"[3] Whereupon, they searched everywhere, went through his identity papers while continuing to call him a Jew. They went as far as forcing him to open his fly and exhibit his genitalia. This was completely crazy!

Two things seemed to condemn David: his name, considered "Jewish" by the Nazis, but also his first name, Emmanuel... Things being what they were, he could find himself in Drancy.

It was necessary to act without delay. Since the brutes involved wore uni-

---

1. An art dealer, discoverer of Carzou and Bernard Buffet whose exclusive representative he was. A former fighter in the two World Wars, he was made Chevalier de la Légion d'honneur. (EdN)

2. A gallery with an international reputation, founded by Emmanuel David and Armand Drouant. Inaugurated in 1942. (EdN)

3. You Jew! in German. (EdN)

forms, they were probably from the S.S. Now, I had neither ties to the Gestapo nor contacts with the S.S. Officers despised the Gestapo, even if I knew its headquarters on avenue Foch. Separated from the other military services during the Occupation, placed under the direct order of Himmler himself, the Gestapo was like a state within a state.

I did not know at all the SS General Oberg. I could have gotten to know him, but I had simply never met him. He was the only one able to save David, because he was the only one holding the authority to formulate a counter-order. Not being a career officer had many disadvantages, but also a few advantages. Since I was not part of the inner circle, I was not impressed by the military hierarchy. Accustomed to dealing with the authorities directly, I would often see the bosses, without first going through the subordinate officers. With Oberg, it was another matter entirely. Before reaching him, it would be necessary to get beyond several guards. Through the official channels, I would have never succeeded. The only card to play was the extra-military one. And it was not negligible. Germans, especially those from the masses, are very impressed by titles, above all university ones. And I was a *Herr Doctor!*

I told poor David to go back home, I put on my uniform, slid my title of doctor in my pocket, and went over to avenue Foch. I made it through the controls with disconcerting ease, and quickly found myself in front of General Oberg. He received me cordially, inquired about my work in Paris and at the Berlin Museum before the war. Since our conversation was unfolding in a friendly manner, I felt that the time had come to get to the point of my visit. In a very solemn and affirmative tone, I told the general that, despite his name, and, also, his first name, not a drop of Jewish blood flowed in David's veins.

Without the slightest hesitation, Oberg reached for the telephone and gave in my presence the orders that stopped in their tracks the procedures set in motion against the "Jew" Emmanuel David. Who, suddenly, was no longer "Jewish."

ANDRÉ SCHOELLER

André Schoeller's renown as an expert was great, mainly for the paintings by Corot. At the Hôtel Drouot, his rank was as important as that of the auctioneers.

Nevertheless, he did not visit with me to talk about painting, but to discuss André Pacitti, on of his illegitimate sons, who had not only inherited his father's first name, but also his taste for painting. At the beginning, he would encourage him in his work, but progressively art assessments also became his specialty. Like many young adults, he had dabbled in the black market, which displeased the German police. Arrested, he was stagnating and sunk in some prison cell or other, along with a number of common criminals. Obviously, his father had come to see me and cry. Someone had told him that I could get him freed easily. But what could I do?

In addition to being a lover of painting, André Schoeller was a great lover of the weaker sex, as one would still refer to it at that time. Mistakenly so, moreover, because he was the one who belonged to the weaker sex. His immoderate taste for women was costing him dearly. According to my information, he had bought himself a house in Paris as an investment which, however, did not bring him any income, since he would lodge his former lady friends free of charge, each one on a different floor.

His last conquest was a very young Russian girl, Nadine, the daughter of Adolf Wüster's [1] wife. Schoeller was already elderly when he married her, far older in any case than his father-in-law. As he died shortly after having been married, malicious gossips said that he had died as a result of it. His wife being much younger than him, the poor old man killed himself on the job.

---

1. A French painter (1888-1972), known for his landscapes and still lifes. (EdN)

I got his son out of jail, but I never saw Schoeller again. No doubt he didn't get arrested again. If that had happened, I would have certainly been entitled to another visit. That's the way it was. What can you do?

ALFRED CORTOT

In September 1942, I learned that my brother had fallen on the Russian front. He was barely 22 years old. My mother being a widow, I was entitled to a leave. It was, nevertheless, refused to me. Without any explanation. But I knew very well what the explanation was. I already knew that certain of my superiors, especially the convinced Nazis, thought that I was not a "good German." For them I was too much of a Francophile, linked too closely to the French, too "friendly" towards them. After the tragic death of my bother, many Parisian friends came to offer me their condolences, among whom was André Dunoyer de Segonzac. [1]

At the same time, Alfred Cortot [2] was preparing an important concert in Berlin. We were very close, and indeed linked by a very warm friendship. When he found out that I had been refused a furlough which was my right, and in so tragic a moment, he had a brilliant idea: he demanded that I accompany him to Berlin where he was invited by his close friend Furtwängler [3] in person.

Given Cortot's European reputation and the fact that the Nazi dignitaries were paying court to him, my superiors could not refuse. A month later, then, Alfred and I were taking the train from the Gare du Nord to Berlin. Thanks to

---

1. A painter, engraver and illustrator (1884-1974). He participated, in November 1941, with other French artists who were among the most renowned, in a "voyage of study" in Germany, organized by Arno Breker. (EdN)

2. Among the most important pianists in the first part of the 20th century, conductor, founder of the École normale de musique in Paris, his official role during the Occupation and his tours in Nazi Germany would considerably sully his reputation and harm his celebrity. (EdN)

3. Wilhelm Furtwängler, a great German conductor, one of the most important in the first half of the 20th century, the legendary director of the Berlin Philharmonic Orchestra. (EdN)

53

Cortot, I would see my mother again, who was devastated by the death of an adored son.

Mama and I met at the Esplanade Hotel, near Potsdam Square. In 1942 that magnificent palace was still operating. We lacked for nothing. Cortot found there, as agreed, the Steinway he had ordered, and not in any hall whatsoever, but in the middle of the salon of his very beautiful suite. For several days, my mother and I had a wonderful time attending Alfred's intense rehearsals. In addition to being a pianist of genius, he was a tireless worker.

On the day of the concert, Philharmonic Hall, still spared by the bombs, was filled to the rafters. Overcome by the emotional reunion with my mother, I had completely forgot to reserve seats. Obviously, there were not any left. Seeing my vexation, Cortot had the two armchairs of his dressing room placed next to his piano! My poor mother, inhibited, but delighted, as one can imagine, attended the concert seated right in the middle of the stage of the Berlin Philharmonic Hall,[4] right beside the master.

Although it was in Berlin, the capital of the Reich, Cortot played only Chopin! With, as a final number, the fabulous sonata in G major, also called The Funeral March. Cortot performed it with such grace and sensibility that at the end of the concert the hall literally exploded in a thunder of applause. My mother was sobbing. Cortot rose, went towards her and took her in his arms, and whispered in her ear: "I have played tonight in honour of your son killed in action, Madame!"

And it was only afterwards that he turned toward the hall where the thunder of applause would rumble for many long minutes.

---

4. The author fails to say, or perhaps he didn't know, that by accepting this tour, Alfred Cortot asked for and received permission to give his first concert, free of charge, at the French Residence of Berlin, then to play for French prisoners. He was the first French musician to perform in Germany after the armistice. His tour was a triumph that would be exploited in France by the collaborationist party. (EdN)

DESPIAU

Charles Despiau [1] lived right next to Montsouris Park, a veritable oasis of calm at that time. I went to see him at his insistent invitation. He absolutely wanted to show me a portrait, that of his doctor in fact, that he was in the process of executing. Many artists then had their studios near the park, in the adjacent little streets. Rousseau, the former Customs Inspector, had already found refuge there. The street of the Customs Inspector bore witness to this as it does today.

In addition to painting, Despiau was a passionate hunter. On entering his studio, I was literally assaulted by a pack of dogs. Agitated but nice, excited by the arrival of a strange visitor, they were running around everywhere, jumping in all directions. All this took place amidst statues, busts, plinths and crates that encumbered the large room. In the middle of this circus, Despiau remained calm and smiling. He maintained that his dogs were so adroit that they never overturned anything.

As skillful as his dogs, small and supple, he also made his way around his works with a disconcerting vivacity, although he was already 70 years old. With his trimmed beard, his cunning gaze, his slightly diabolical smile, he looked like a real little satyr! Half young and half old, half man and half faun.

The purpose of my visit was on a plinth, covered over as it should be with a damp cloth. Despiau unveiled it carefully and I was immediately struck by the incredible resemblance to the model. Because I knew the doctor in question. Everything was there: the physical, the psychological, the spirit. Most sculptors make recognizable portraits, but dead ones. Only the great ones manage

---

1. A French sculptor of international renown (1874-1946) who influenced numerous artists, including Paul Belmondo. (EdN)

to make matter come alive: clay, then cold bronze. The traits were certainly simplified. It was a work by Despiau, but the most important element was there: life!

He had needed fifty sessions to arrive at this result. The portrait was now completed. Despiau worked slowly. Everyone knew it. Since Rudier was going to take charge of casting this bust, one could be sure in advance that it would be a marvel. This was, moreover, a beautiful story. Despiau was not going to sell this portrait, but offer it to his doctor as thanks for having taken such good care of him, and... free of charge! This doctor had indeed always refused to accept payment from Despiau, who followed to the letter the treatments prescribed, with one exception: he could not stop smoking. This vice caused him serious problems in a period of restrictions. Trying to get hold of cigarettes could become a full-time occupation.

Since recognition came late for him, Despiau had remained a modest man, worried by material concerns. He also kept his "workman" demeanor, a throwback no doubt to the beginning of his career in Rodin's studios, where he would execute his master's marble portraits.

During one of Dina Vierny's [2] rare stays in Paris, we decided to spend the Sunday in Robinson, to escape the Parisian heat. I was a great admirer of Maillol and I like Dina, his muse, very much. We wanted to have lunch at chez Blandeau, a little country restaurant which Rudier enjoyed particularly. One could always find something there to eat, and one could eat well. The train which was leaving from the Luxembourg station in the direction of Sceaux, was filled to capacity. One would have thought that the whole of Paris was fleeing the furnace in the capital. To help the time pass, we were chatting about various matters, without any specific purpose. We talked about Rudier, Maillol and Despiau. Dina liked Despiau very much and was worried about his health. The last time she had seen him, he appeared to her very tired, as though he were suffering from an illness.

And I replied, laughing:

"Not at all, he isn't sick. You know his cousin? He has a crush on her. She's the one who is tiring him out from what I hear."

Dina burst out laughing. But scarcely had I pronounced these words than a lady, visibly annoyed, interjected in a loud voice:

"These are nothing but lies! I'm the one who is Despiau's cousin!"

---

2. Of Russian origin, she was Maillol's model and inspiration (1919-2009), a well-known gallery owner, and the founder of the Musée Maillol in Paris. (EdN)

Astonishment! As a precautionary measure, we continued our conversation in German. Dina spoke it very well, because, as a little child, she had had a German governess. While we were talking, she stared at that woman.

At the restaurant, she told me that the woman was really Despiau's cousin. Dina had remembered seeing her in the studio, during the period when she posed for him.

Despiau was an eminently kindly man, friendly, and loved by everybody. Unfortunately for him, careless about things and heedless of political implications, he had joined his more famous colleagues and took part, as well, in the famous voyage of French artists to Germany. We will refer to this matter further on. But in addition, contrary to others, he had agreed to be listed in the catalogue of the Arno Breker exhibition, with a text signed in due form.

Stigmatized as a "collaborator" after the war, the poor man was so affected by this that it lead to his death.

DUFY

During a trip to Banyuls which I will talk about further on, [1] I had paid a visit to Raoul Dufy, settled in Perpignan since the exodus. I don't know if it is because of me or not, but the fact remains that in the spring of 1944, Dufy returned to his studio in Montmartre which had remained empty and uninhabited for four years. To the left of the Impasse Guelma, the street that goes down from the boulevard de Clichy, stood a rather large house, with its studios. Dufy had been settled there since 1911. [2] Both his apartment and studio were there.

We had an appointment. He welcomed me warmly and led me right away into his studio, at the end of a vestibule, which overlooked both the street and the courtyard.

Unlike in Perpignan, where he was in excellent health, I found him suffering agony because of his rheumatisms, to the point of no longer being able to walk. Not really, in any case.

To my great surprise, piles of paintings were stacked up in the workshop. Paintings from every period. We had looked for a long time at drawings and, especially, watercolours of which I had seen the sketches in Perpignan: harvests, threshing machines.

Dufy cared a great deal about the conception, indeed the composition and production of his colours. Fascinated by the ancient techniques, especially Grünewald's, which he had closely studied, he dreamt of attaining the same luminosity as his master, and the same clarity.

On the back of each painting, he would inscribe a mysterious number which

---

1. In 1943. (EdN)

2. On the first floor of the building. (EdN)

corresponded to a formula. A number that he listed in a notebook, which was accompanied by a detailed, explanatory description written down very diligently. For every new painting he would use a new formula, sometimes changing the technique three or four times for the same subject.

While we were looking at the different works, notably prints painted on wood, a man who had remained silent up till then in a corner of the studio, came over to join our conversation. Dufy introduced us. It was his chemist. Without beating around the bush, the man explained to me at length the way he worked. He would mix the different colours in powder form so skillfully and conscientiously with the oils and filler that, without intending to, I saw in him the co-author, still unknown today, of Dufy's works.

KEES VAN DONGEN

Every time he came to see me, Kees van Dongen would speak to me about Holland. His Parisian success and world-wide glory did not blur his desire to see his country again. He would dream of tulip fields. He often talked about their colours, yellow and especially red, and yearned to be able one day to see them from high above.

He wanted me to help him organize an aerial view of the tulip fields, whereas he knew that this was totally impossible because of the war.

It was literally in clogs that Kees had landed in Paris, young, tall, a handsome kid, but without a cent. He had known poverty, had frequented dropouts, slept in trailers, and mixed with a shady, dangerous crowd. Since he was a strapping young man, he worked for a while as a "strong guy" at the Halles market, carried beef carcasses; then, as a painter in the construction trade. Every job was good enough for him, he accepted any one. And he put aside every cent that he could. And this is how, thanks to his paltry savings, he succeeded in constituting a little kitty. This allowed him eventually to leave the slum belt and set himself up in Montmartre. From that moment on, he did nothing else but paint. Influenced, probably too much so, by the "fauves" of Chatou.

And it worked! Barely several years later, there he was a society painter, this time residing in the heart of Paris. His feminine portraits, fireworks of silks, jewels, brilliant colours and having a loud elegance, gave enormous pleasure. His women with their mannered facial expressions were like dolls with eyes painted and lips made up in red and blue. Rich and adulated, Kees van Dongen had become *the* portraitist of high society.

The Charpentier Gallery had decided to organize a large exhibition—almost a retrospective--of his work. [1] All the socialites and elegant ladies of Paris would find one another again on the walls of the gallery. It would be their triumph, too. The rare male portraits by van Dongen represented Anatole France, the Aga Khan and Boniface de Castellane.

His large studio, on boulevard de Courcelles, looked more like a film sound stage. There were so many projectors in this hall the ceiling of which was very high. In that space would unfold the famous "van Dongen parties" in which everyone wanted to be included and what everyone in Paris was talking about.

I would see him from time to time, almost as a neighbour, always with a box of oil colours in my hand. He had trouble obtaining them in this period of restrictions, especially white which he greatly needed, and in large quantities, because of the jewels with which he adorned "his women." As a way of thanking me, van Dongen rewarded me with a smile that illuminated his handsome aristocratic head in a truly astonishing way.

One day, he showed me the portrait he was preparing of Mme Utrillo, better known under the name of " Kind Lucie," decked out in all the contents of his jewel box. He was unable to paint it, he told me, for lack of the colour white. So I arrived in the nick of time.

---

1. In 1943. (EdN)

THE THREE SISTERS, BUTTER AND PICASSO

On the rue Dauphine, not far from the Pont Neuf, was an old, charmless shop, with its shutters always closed, and with its front entrance blocked by a thick wooden plank. Everything about it was dirty and the whole building gave a clear impression of being abandoned. Nevertheless, all one had to do was knock three times for this door to open and reveal a fat, curly head that assessed you silently before letting you enter. It was necessary, of course, to be known and recognized. Once one passed over the threshold, one found oneself in a dimly lit room, filled with tables and chairs. It was a hidden little restaurant, where one could eat incredible things to one's heart's content: pâtés, roasts, choux à la crème... Everything that one could not find anywhere! The privileged people who frequented this really magical place, this culinary refuge with a simple and convivial atmosphere, had baptized it "three sisters, three beautiful asses." Because, naturally, of the three sisters who ran it, three fat women, with physical appearances typical of "the women of the Halles market."

The first sister took care of the entrées, the second did the roasts, as for the third who suffered from rheumatisms that prevented her from walking, she remained seated in front of the pastry oven. And her pastries were really exquisite. Their brother, Raymond, the lazybones of the family, a man with a dumb-looking face, was banned from the kitchen, and even from the ground floor. He had to remain in the room on the first floor, without doing anything. All day long, he did nothing except fiddle with the buttons on his radio, to listen to the BBC. And he did this, knowing that the establishment was frequented by Germans! Raymond couldn't have cared less. When I went up to the floor to greet him, I was often welcomed by the famous three chords of

Beethoven's Fifth Symphony, followed by news of "la France libre" (Free France). It didn't even occur to him that what he did might displease me.

Well connected to the black market, the three sisters never lacked for anything. This explains why they had so many faithful clients. One day, however, they were out of butter. There was utter despair! The Normandy farmer, their supplier, had indeed brought a fat package of it, but for fear of a city toll, he had not crossed into Paris itself and was now at the Porte Maillot, not daring to face German inspection. The sisters looked at me in a supplicating way, their eyes overflowing with hope. But I could not, in any circumstances, take on this task. So everything seemed lost until one of the guests had a brilliant idea. His brother, he told us, was stationed at the Vieux Colombier firemen's barracks, very close, at the time, to where we were situated. The German guards never stopped and never inspected the firemen's trucks. The good man quickly asked his brother to make a round trip to Neuilly, in exchange for the promise of a delicious meal. One hour later, we could hear the firemen's siren coming up the rue Dauphine in the direction of the Buci crossroad. The Normandy butter had arrived.

One evening, in 1943, I was having dinner at the famous Three sister's place with Maratier. We had barely finished giving our order when there were three knocks at the door. Some new customers were coming in, among them Picasso and Dora Maar, along with their Afghan hound. Maratier who was on a first name basis with "Pablo"—they were genuine friends--was so happily surprised that he invited them to join us. Obviously, he did the introductions in such a way that Picasso knew exactly who I was.

The dinner was very agreeable. I had never met Dora Maar. I had seen only the portraits that Picasso had made of her as well as her sculpted bust. She was not talkative, dressed all in black, distant, stiff, beautiful,—really very beautiful—with regular features and very black hair. Exotic. I knew she came from the fringes of Yugoslavia. This was obvious: her face bore her Slavic origins.

The bulk of the conversation occurred between Picasso and Maratier. They had known each other forever. They talked a great deal about their close friend, Gertrude Stein, of their voyages, of everything, in short, except Picasso's work. While conversing with me, Picasso was putting on an act, as though I had been a mere guest.

Once a month, a meeting of artists took place at the Three Sisters'. With copious libations, it goes without saying. That particular evening was one of them. We were still seated at our table when they were already coming down one after the other. Othon Friesz the painter, Mayodon the ceramist, Subes the art blacksmith. I knew all of them. And they also knew me, just as they knew Picasso. But seeing us at our table, me the "Nazi" and him the "red pet hate" of the Nazis, troubled them so much that they disappeared very quickly, using the curfew as a pretext. I could guess what would happen. The next morning, the elegant set of Paris would hear about it, and the price of Picasso's paintings would rise.

After this amusing interlude, we went to have coffee at Maratier's, who lived a few steps from the restaurant, on the Quai de l'Horloge, right opposite the Court House. Maratier's salon was crammed with drawings and paintings, including some very beautiful nudes by Picasso. Pablo curiously examined the other artists works, one after the other, but conspicuously ignored his own.

The hour was late. Curfew was approaching. Picasso looked at the time, then addressed me with a mischievous smile.

"Sir," he said to me, "We must leave, curfew oblige. Otherwise, as you well know, the Germans are going to arrest us."

Everyone laughed. He knew how to be funny!

Of all the living artists, Pablo Picasso was certainly the one the Nazis detested most. He was *the* uncontested star of the famous exhibition "degenerate art" that was touring just about everywhere in Germany. An avowed enemy of Franco and friend of the Spanish republicans, Picasso was considered a communist sympathizer, and his painting Guernica was viewed as openly "anti-German," since it was the German Condor division that had bombarded this little Spanish town.

Contrary to Chagall and others, Picasso had remained in Paris, and continued living and working at his home, on the rue des Grands Augustins. If Picasso had demonstrated politically in one way or another, I would have had to bear down on him, in conformity with the instructions I received. But as long as he kept quiet, as long as he didn't really show his political colours, I didn't have to intervene. Moreover, his dealer, Henri Kahnweiler, having left Paris, and for good reason, Picasso was not exhibiting and so didn't have to deal with me.

Kahnweiler had already been obliged to leave France, in 1914, because he was a German. And his wealth was confiscated. He returned to Paris after the First World War, but could not recover anything, because the Republic had auctioned off everything. This time, Kahnweiler had left France because he was a Jew. But he took his precautions. His gallery was officially the property of his faithful collaborator and sister-in-law, Louise Leiris, who didn't have a drop of Jewish blood. The Leiris Gallery avoided organizing events, drawing attention to itself, and its owner showed great caution. There was no reason for me to go there. So I never went there. It was better that way.

Nevertheless, I had to "deal with" Picasso for the good and simple reason that Martin Fabiani, an art dealer and editor of high quality books, was preparing a new edition of the "Buffon" that he wanted to enhance—a funny idea--with engravings by Picasso. It was not my job to get involved in editorial decisions as such, but for the publication of this book, my signature was required, if not indispensable. This presented a moral dilemma for me: on the one hand I liked Picasso very much; on the other I was a German officer and consequently I had to obey orders. A minimum in any event... And the present case was more difficult than the previous one, because Dr. Piersig of the Embassy had telephoned me to share with me a letter of information received from Berne, saying that Skira was preparing the publication of a book devoted to Picasso's works. Edited in Switzerland, the volume was then to be sold clandestinely in France. Having listened to him attentively, I asked Dr. Piersig if there was a wastepaper basket in his office, and I invited him to throw the letter there. This time, I could not escape so easily.

REMEMBERING THE NABIS

Maurice Denis is the one who best described the Nabis position, by saying that "every work of art was a transposition, an impassioned equivalent, and a caricature of sensations received." Among the young Nabis of the period were Redon, Vuillard, Maurice Denis, Sérusier, Ranson, Roussel, Bonnard, the art dealer Vollard and also Madame Denis. They considered themselves as "Nabis," in other word, prophets. Prophets of what, I cannot say. They probably knew. A short while after the creation of the group, two others joined them: the very great Swiss painter Vallotton and, above all, my friend Aristide Maillol who was still interested in painting.

As I have already mentioned, I believe, in 1943 Maillol lived with me at the Hôtel Lincoln, on the rue Bayard. Aristide enjoyed talking at breakfast, but especially during the long evenings that we spent together. He could talk forever. Particularly, about his early years as a painter. And even though, over the past forty years, he did nothing but sculpture, he remained, as he said, faithful to the "Nabis", to their research, to his friends Vuillard, Denis and Roussel. Maillol was a remarkable and unpredictable man. For example, he had refused to execute the frescos of the Théâtre des Champs-Élysées, on the pretext that the time allotted him was not long enough, even though the commission was prestigious and very lucrative. The sculptor Antoine Bourdelle didn't find the time too short, and he carried out the work in Maillol's place.

Maillol's home in Marly was, moreover, a reflection of that period of his life. All the paintings of his friends were hanging on the walls. I will never forget Gauguin's large seascape which he showed me one day, as though it was the most ordinary thing in the world. It was extraordinary!

Maillol was particularly friendly with K.X. Roussel, [1] his neighbour at Étang-la-Ville. The latter often came to Marly with his children, Jacques and Annette, who would play with the young Lucien Maillol. Aristide would also frequently pay visits to the Roussels who had built themselves a spacious bourgeois home surrounded by a sumptuous park. And then there was also his neighbour, Mme de Waard, nicknamed "Be", whom Maillol admired, just as did Rilke in his time. She would lead Maillol "into discussions that were more than spiritual." This is what he maintained at any rate.

These chats with Maillol gave me the agreeable impression of living the history of art from within, of being there without being part of it. Besides, I often found myself taking notes once I went back up to my room.

Maillol was fond of K.X. Roussel, adhered with all his heart to the ideas of the Nabis, and yet did not like Maurice Denis very much. He acknowledged, of course, the latter's role as the founder and theoretician of the movement. He admired "his definition of neo-traditionalism" but added right away that Denis worked more with his pen than with his paintbrush. That he wrote more than he painted. In addition, he did not like at all the way Maurice Denis was shifting towards religious painting, with its pale pink and blue colours.

One day, to my great surprise, he nevertheless suggested that we take the train to Saint-Germain-en-Laye from the Saint-Lazare train station, to say hello to his former friend, Maurice Denis, who had become in the meantime a member of the Institut. Alas, we could not realize this project, because Maurice Denis died several days later, in a traffic accident at Place Saint Michel. Maillol was very affected by this and wanted to know the details. At his request, I questioned the police who told me that he had died "foolishly." After leaving the Institut, Maurice Denis had walked along the Quai Conti and was getting ready to change sidewalks at Place Saint Michel, when a sudden gust of wind blew up his long cape and blinded him. Thus he did not see the truck coming at him at high speed and was killed on the spot.

So instead of going to visit Maurice Denis, we attended his burial.

---

1. François-Xavier Roussel, called Ker-Xavier Roussel (1867-1944), a member of the Nabis group, nicknamed "Bucolic Nabi" because of his penchant for nature. (EdN)

THE TRIP TO GERMANY

I don't know who thought of it first, but the fact remained that we received the order from Berlin to organize an official trip to Germany that would, if I may say so, get media coverage. The idea was to get together a group of great French artists, then to cart them across the Third Reich. The Ministry of Propaganda and Dr. Goebbels in person were very keen about it. So it was out of the question to discuss or shirk it. Otto Abetz, our ambassador, took charge of the matter personally and drew up a list of people whom it would be necessary now to convince to embark on the trip. He succeeded on that score without difficulty, with only two exceptions: Maurice Vlaminck and André Derain. Not that they were opposed to the idea of a trip to Germany. Not at all. They were simply mad at one another.

When I met them, Derain and Vlaminck had not seen one another in years. Their friendship, although very old, had run out of steam several years before my arrival in Paris. They had broken off totally, to Vlaminck's great regret, as he told me himself. Their quarrel had nothing really nasty about it. I had heard about it from both sides. They were both very stubborn men, that was all.

Vlaminck used to visit Derain often at home. The latter lived at the time at 31 rue Bonaparte. André, who had always loved the theatre in all its forms, was working then for the Ballets Russes. Diaghilev had asked him to design the sets for a production, and it was taking a lot of time. Seeing his friend so absorbed by the theatre that he was no longer painting, Vlaminck, who had a big mouth, told him in an enervated tone: "You are no longer a painter, but a ballerina!" Derain took it the wrong way, so that spelled the end of their friendship, whereas beforehand they had been inseparable.

I am speaking about it here, because their quarrel would cause me problems, since I was entrusted with the practical part of this famous trip to Germany. In principle, this trip was no big deal. The delegation of French artists were supposed to visit several museums and pay visits to German artists. Nothing remarkable, then, nor openly political. Since they were well-known and admired across the Rhine, Vlaminck and Derain absolutely had to be there. They had to agree to take the same train no matter what. I got down to work on it with the best intentions in the world. After many efforts, I succeeded in dragging out of them a vague agreement in theory, but not in reconciling them. Even though I thought I had managed to do so at one given moment. With Vlaminck, it was still possible, but Derain remained closed-mouthed. Neither an outright refusal, nor a clear acceptance. This was dangerous.

The more time was passing, the more Berlin was insisting on these two names explicitly. Abetz was insisting more and more strenuously. Things even went much further. During a crisis meeting at the Ritz (masquerading as a social reception) the Commandant of Paris [1] himself made the effort to be there. This underscored the importance of the thing. In the face of such a "deployment of troops," Derain and Vlaminck had no other choice but to reconcile.

The list was complete: Vlaminck, Derain, Legueult, Despiau, Othon Friesz, Dunoyer de Ségonzac, van Dongen, Oudot, Landowski and Belmondo. In the end, no one had refused. Some had perhaps accepted for fear of getting into trouble, but others went willingly. After the war, the participants in this famous trip were accused of "collaboration" and some were arrested. Admittedly, no one was really obligated to go there, but artists are rarely clever politically. Maillol, who, of all people, could have been accused of "collaboration," flatly refused the invitation, even though Berlin was very anxious for him to be present. The reply he had sent me was clear and crisp: "I know Germany. I visited it with Count Kessler!"

In principle, and given my functions, I should have been in charge of this trip. But because it was considered of utmost importance by the Nazi propaganda machine, I was pushed aside, thank God, in favour of people whose rank was higher than mine, and who were eager to get the attention.

It was perhaps also because I had publically raised questions, from the very beginning of the preparations for the trip, about what could possibly interest these French artists in Germany. What could one show them that was capable

---

1. General Otto von Stülpnagel, Chief of the German Occupation Forces in France and Military Governor of Paris from 1941 to 1942. Arrested after the war, he was transferred to Paris to be judged, but committed suicide in 1948 at the Cherche-Midi prison. (EdN)

of impressing them and to whom could one introduce them? The expression-
ists no longer existed! Either dead or emigrated. And those who had remained
in Germany could neither exhibit nor appear in public. Now these were the
only ones known in France. The exaggerated big nude paintings by an Adolf
Ziegler, [2] an official painter that the state exhibited everywhere, could only
elicit embarrassed smiles among French artists.

The program for the trip began with a visit to the new Chancellery of the
Reich, then continued with a ride to Wriezen, east of Berlin, where Arno Breker received everyone and took them on a guided tour of his oversized "State
Studios" where he produced his almost unimaginably gigantic sculptures, destined to adorn the immense avenues of the "New Berlin." Although totally
"official" and adhering to the ideas of the Third Reich, Arno Breker was one of
the rare artists active in Germany who was respected by his foreign colleagues
for the quality of his work. For example, Salvador Dali would acquire the very
beautiful portrait of Jean Cocteau that Arno Breker had painted after the war. [3]
After Berlin, the group was unfortunately taken to Munich, to see the studio of
the pretentious portraitist, Leo Samberger. [4]

After the Liberation, Derain had the problems one can imagine, and very
big ones! It got to the point that he abandoned his studio on the rue d'Assas,
and withdrew definitively to Chambourcy. Desperate and broken, he continued
painting without ever regaining his peace of mind, as much because of the
persecutions as of Alice, who became, as she aged, a veritable torturer. It was
very difficult for me to imagine this as I knew her to be so kind, and even so
adorable.

Unlike André, her husband, a real giant, Alice was petite and tubby. As a
young woman, she apparently looked like a little Madonna with blue eyes and
a thick head of hair.

From the time she was seven years old according to some, little Alice
cohabited with a certain Princet, a civil servant, who, believe it or not, one

---

2. Hitler's preferred painter, entrusted by the former to purify German painting of "degenerate
artists", Adolf Ziegler (1892-1959) was named a Senator for Fine Arts by the Reich, and became
in 1936 President of the Reich Chamber for the Arts. (EdN)

3. The work is exhibited in the museum-home of Salvador Dali in Cadaquès, in Catalonia.
(EdN)

4. A Munich painter, Leo Samberger (1861-1949) was one of the signatories of the Declaration
of German artists against Bolshevik, Masonic and Jewish art, published in 1933 and directed
particularly against Emil Nolde, Paul Klee and Ludwig Mies van der Rohe. (EdN)

fine day decided nonetheless to take her as his wife. For fear of losing her, no doubt. Except that it was too late. The girl had already been frequenting artists. Notably in the circle of Fernande Olivier, [5] who told her: "Why get married? To get divorced?" She didn't know how right she was. Very soon, Alice met André Derain, and left her Princet notwithstanding the fact that she had married him.

One day, it must have been in 1941, Alice Derain, whom people called "la môme Alice (Little Alice), came to see me because when she returned to Paris after the exodus, she found the Derains' large property occupied by German troops. [6] Since she couldn't make them leave, she came to ask my help in finding a suitable dwelling in the Saint-Germain-des-Prés area. She knew that many apartments remained empty in the elegant neighbourhoods. Astonishingly, she didn't come alone, but with little Bobby, the child that André had produced as a result of a relationship with Raymonde, his model. This simple fact showed to what extent she was a good soul. Because the relationship between André and Raymonde had upset the Derain couple.

Although he lived with Alice in the country, Derain had retained his studio in Paris, opposite the Luxembourg garden. [7] He had the peace and quiet, he said, to work, and also to take care of his kid. I often went there. He had set up there a private little corner, decorated with a provincial landscape that reminded him of his years as a fauve painter, with little still life paintings, with statues made of iron and terra cotta (research in sculpture preoccupied him a great deal at that time). For the rest, the studio was Bobby's domain. The little boy had a large and beautiful marionette theatre at his disposal, crates filled with dolls that Durain had dressed himself, and moreover, whose heads he had sculpted. Bobby had a good time with this theatre, to his father's great joy.

Having known Alice as such a good soul, I could not imagine her terrorizing André who had become vulnerable after the torments of the purge. For example, she would dare to kick up gigantic fusses on the pretext that he "was squandering her money," even though she had never earned a cent. Unfortunately for André, they had been married with a communal estate settlement.

---

5. Her real name was Amélie Lang. Fernande Olivier was the companion of Guillaume Apollinaire and Pablo Picasso, at the beginning of his rose then cubist period, between 1904 and 1912. (EdN)

6. In Chambourcy, near Saint-Germain-en-Laye. (EdN)

7. At 112 rue d'Assas. (EdN)

These incessant quarrels were so violent that they finally affected Derain's mind. Especially when the *môme* had all his wealth seized. With the complicity of a prejudiced judge, no doubt. He no longer owned his home, and so he no longer had the right to touch anything. Even his paintbrushes. The situation was crazy.

Shortly after this truly scandalous seizure, a small truck knocked down a haggard André near his home. That was in 1954.

In conformity with Alice's wishes, the burial took place in the strictest intimacy, and went unnoticed.

Werner Lange in his office at the *Propagandastaffel*. (Private Collection)

Cécile Sorel returns to Paris. Photo taken in front of the Hôtel Bristol, on the rue du Faubourg Saint-Honoré. (Private Collection)

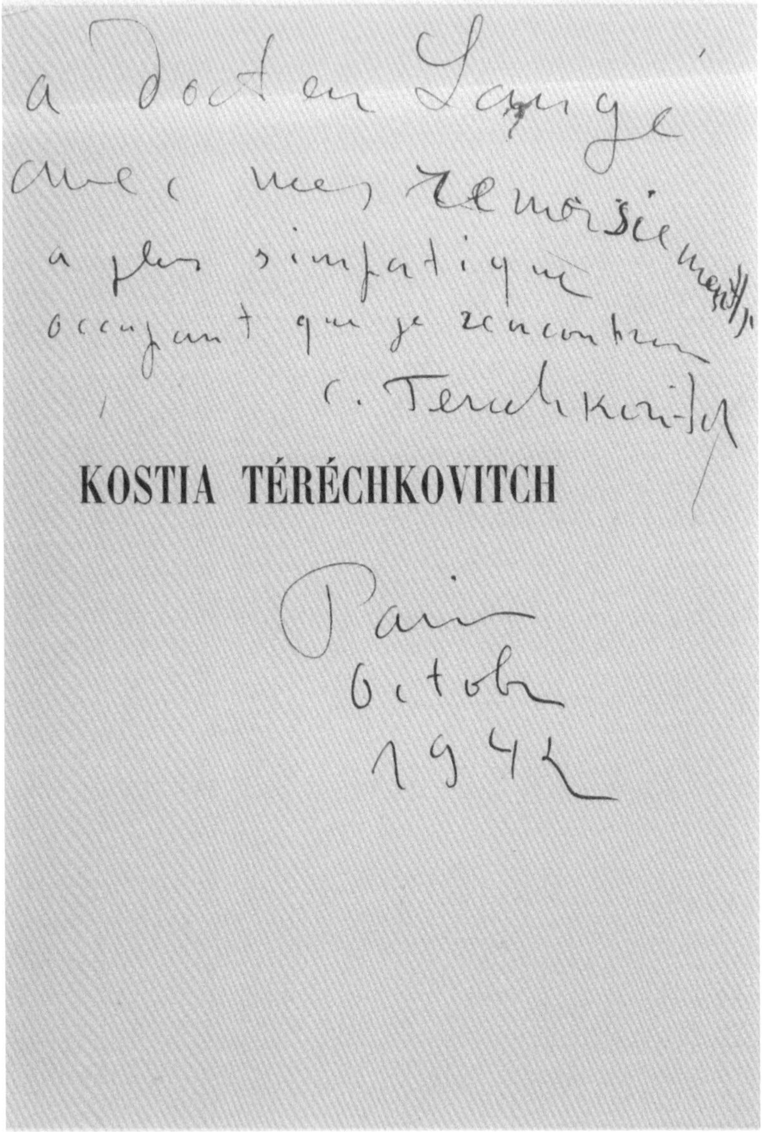

à docteur Lange
avec mes témoignages
à plus sympathique
occupant que je rencontre
C. Teréchkovitch

KOSTIA TÉRÉCHKOVITCH

Paris
Octobre
1942

Dedication of the book *Kostia Téréchkovitch* by Louis Chevronnet,
published by Éditions Sequana. (Private Collection)

Photo autographed by Alfred Cortot for Dr. Werner Lange. (Private
Collection)

Charles Despiau (Private Collection)

Charles Despiau in his studio. (Private Collection)

Dina Vierny, photo taken by Werner Lange. (Private Collection)

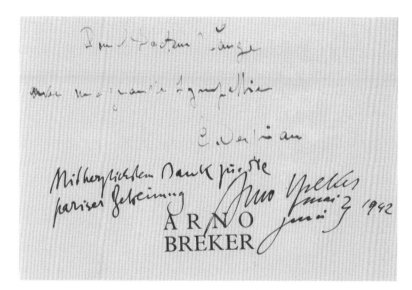

The catalogue of Arno Breker's Parisian exhibition published by the Éditions Flammarion, autographed for Werner Lange by Charles Despiau and Arno Breker (Private Collection).

Return from Germany, Gare de l'Est station. In the foreground, from left to right: Despiau (the second, with his hands in his pockets), Friesz de Vlaminck, van Dongen (with the white beard) and, at the extreme right, Lieutenant Lucht (in a leather coat). In the second row, between Vlaminck and van Dongen, the editor Henri Flammarion. (Private Collection)

Maurice de Vlaminck in his famous brown sagging armchair. Photo by
Werner Lange taken at La Tourillière in 1942. (Private Collection)

Berthe, Edwige and Maurice de Vlaminck at La Tourillière, 1942. Photo
taken by Werner Lange. (Private Collection)

Maurice de Vlaminck showing his canvases to Werner Lange. La Tourillière, 1942. Photo taken by Werner Lange. (Private Collection)

Maurice de Vlaminck and Werner Lange at La Tourillière, 1942. Photo
taken by Edwige de Vlaminck. (Private Collection)

Eugène Rudier, foundry owner. (Private Collection)

The Rudier Foundry, 1942. On the wall, the plaster model of Diana reclining with the stag by Benvenuto Cellini, cast for Goering in 1941. Photo taken by Werner Lange. (Private Collection)

Eugène Rudier standing next to a work by Arno Breker, cast in his workshop. Photo taken by Werner Lange. (Private Collection)

Eugène Rudier and Werner Lange standing in front of a work by Arno
Breker. (Private Collection)

Maurice Utrillo's dedication to Werner Lange, in the catalogue of his
recent works, exhibited at the Galerie Pétridès, from April 18 to May 10,
1942. (Private Collection)

Guillaume Apollinaire, in 1917. (Private Collection)

Georges Maratier, Werner Lange and Jacqueline Apollinaire, after the war.
(Private Collection)

Gertrude Stein and Alice B. Toklas, before the war. (Private Collection)

Portrait of Gertrude Stein by Pablo Picasso. Photo taken by Man Ray.
(Private Collection)

Gertrude Stein's emblem, with her motto: «*A rose is a rose...* « With the
initials «GS» for Gertrude Stein and «AT» for Alice Toklas. A work made
of silver-lined paper, offered by Gertrude Stein to Werner Lange. (Private
Collection)

The Galerie Maratier, at 20 Place Vendôme. (Private Collection)

First floor of the Galerie Maratier, with in the background a painting by
K.X. Roussel. (Private Collection)

Aristide Maillol in Banyuls, 1943. Photo taken by Werner Lange. (Private Collection)

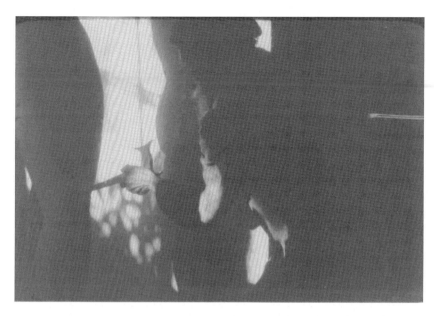

Aristide Maillol working on the plaster model of L'Harmonie with a saw.
Banyuls, 1942. Photo taken by Werner Lange. (Private Collection)

Banyuls, 1942. Photo taken by Werner Lange. (Private Collection)

Werner Lange in Nice, 1942. (Private Collection)

Werner Lange (in uniform, full-frontal) accompanying Aristide and
Clotilde Maillol at the inauguration of Arno Breker's Exhibition at the
Orangerie. Paris, 1942. (Private Collection)

Inauguration of the exhibition of Arno Breker's works, at the Orangerie, in the Tuileries gardens. Opening speech by Abel Bonard, the Minister of Education. In the first row, from left to right: Mimina Breker, Arno Breker, Fernand de Brinon, General Barkhausen, the Gauleiter Fritz Saucke, the Ambassador Otto Abetz. In the second row, between Mimina and Arno Breker, one recognizes Serge Lifar and Jean Cocteau. (Private Collection)

Wilhelm Kempf and Alfred Cortot, in concert on May 15 1942, at the inauguration of the exhibition of Arno Breker's works, at the Orangerie, in the Tuileries gardens. (Private Collection)

Arno Breker, Charles Despiau, Aristide Maillol and Louis Hautecoeur
at the inauguration of Arno Breker's exhibition, at the Orangerie. Paris,
1942. (Private Collection)

Arno Breker, René d'Uckermann and Claude Flammario at La Tronche.
October 1943. Photo taken by Werner Lange. (Private Collection)

René d'Uckermann, Mimina Breker, the Prefect of the Isère, Arno Breker and Claude Flammarion at La Tronche. October 1943. Photo taken by Werner Lange. (Private Collection)

Aristide Maillol posing for Arno Breker. On the left, the plaster model of l'Harmonie. Banyuls, 1943. (Private Collection)

Arno Breker working on the bust of Aristide Maillol. Banyuls, 1943. Photo taken by Werner Lange. (Private Collection)

Clotilde Maillol and Mimina Breker, Banyuls 1943. Photo taken by
Werner Lange. (Private Collection)

Dina Vierny and Werner Lange on the terrace of the *Propagandastaffel* building, on the Champs-Élysées. (Private Collection)

AFTER THE TRIP

Barely a few days after his return from Germany, I paid a visit to André Derain. I didn't have any particular business to arrange with him, I was simply curious to hear about his impressions. "It was long, very long," he told me. "And everything was at a breakneck pace. My son is happy with the toys I brought back for him from Nuremberg. And if he is happy, I'm happy too. There you have it!"

This being said, it was not necessary for me to move about a lot, because the artists who had participated in the tour passed through my office one after the other during the days that followed their return. And they did not come with empty hands. Each one brought a work, and sometimes two or three. Someone had suggested to them to thank Dr. Goebbels for such a lovely trip.

Vlaminck arrived with a very beautiful gouache that represented a Holland landscape. Segonzac brought a magnificent Provencal drawing. Derain dug up from his studio a splendid sanguine representing a woman standing. In short, I suddenly had in my office a collection which would have made any informed collector grow pale with envy, and, in addition, very representative of the best French art of the period.

These masterpieces were still laying around in my office, there is no other word to describe it, when René d'Uckermann [1] from Flammarion came to see me about the publishing business. Very impressed, he told me that what this magnificent ensemble lacked was an attractive presentation: a passe-partout and a gift box in beautiful leather. He very kindly offered the services of the Éditions Flammarion to take charge of this. I accepted with joy, happy to be rid of that chore, and also because I knew that it would be done well. Flammarion

---

1. The literary director of the éditions Flammarion. (EdN)

was truly a very significant publishing house. The gifts were so numerous that it was necessary to make several trips by car to transport all of these works to number 26 rue Racine. [2]

With the passing of time, I had never really taken the matter in hand; then I had to leave Paris. I have often thought back to this situation, while hoping that those gifts offered so naively to Goebbels would not be used as evidence against them, during the trials that all these great artists had to go through after the war.

In all honesty, I don't know what became of those art works.

---

2. The historic headquarters of the Editions Flammarion which the publishing house left since then. (EdN)

LA TOURILLIÈRE

One Saturday morning, on a very busy day in the office, I heard cries coming from the corridor. The voice of the screamer was immediately recognizable: it was Vlaminck, abusing the office boy profusely, a young and meticulous Frenchman. "You prick!" was, in the torrent, the most moderate of the insults. He had come to Paris to see Metthey, [1] and had climbed up the five floors just to say hello to me, and there was the poor boy, seated at the entrance, too zealous no doubt, asking him to fill out a visitor card. This procedure was compulsory in principle, but was implemented very casually, given the fact that Vlaminck was such a celebrity.

Vlaminck was howling as he was advancing in the corridor, and the poor boy, livid, was running behind him, with the bloody little card in his hand.

"You see," he said to me, flopping into an armchair, "Paris is no longer liveable! It is hell. There is too much noise. One can no longer speak. In my place, it is peaceful. Come to La Tourillière, the whole family is waiting for you."

Very happy for this kind invitation, I telephoned the Vlamincks to announce my arrival as early as the following week. Vlaminck had a horror of "all these modern gadgets," and never answered the telephone himself. So his wife was the one I had on the line, and she explained to me in minute detail how to get to Verneuil. Her daughter Edwige would wait for me at the station.

Despite the changes and transfers, the trip was not very long, and Edwige was waiting for me, as planned, in the car. We went first to fetch Godeline, her sister, who was doing the shopping. Then the young ladies insisted on

---

1. André Metthey, a very active art dealer under the Occupation. The owner of the Élysée Gallery. (EdN)

stopping at the bistro, to have a drink with their friends. I had no other choice but to follow them. All these delays must have enervated Vlaminck quite a bit, because he was standing in the courtyard waiting for us. And for more than a little while, apparently. We had barely arrived when he wanted everyone to sit down at the table. I knew he was a big eater, but I didn't know that the sensation of hunger put him in a bad mood. Berthe would explain this to me later. So we went without delay to the dining room filled almost entirely by a long table with benches just as long on either side of it. Feeling guilty for having taken so long, the girls set the table very quickly. One should say rather that they loaded the table with several earthenware vessels filled with pâtés, all of which were delicious. There was more than one enormous piece of meat, the sight of which was incredible in that period of restrictions!

Seated in front of the genial Vlaminck, a real patriarch of French painting, I said to myself that no one could imagine, on seeing the imposing, impressive head of La Tourillière, that at the beginning he had been a poor little boy from Le Vésinet.

Of Flemish origin, coming from a modest family—his grandmother was a vegetable vendor--Vlaminck was not at all an aristocrat. His particle came from the Flemish language, and it was simply the definite article "the." His "difficult" character was, they said, "typically Flemish." The Flemish who had struggled so hard for their independence, were supposed to have a rebellious, libertarian temperament, opposed to everything. From his youth as a furious anarchist, close to terrorists, Vlaminck had retained an angry, explosive personality that was the cause of many break-ups, including the one with his old and dear friend Derain. Married at eighteen years old, he had three daughters from this first marriage that lasted nonetheless twenty-five years, even though he never spoke about it. Vlaminck was already painting at the time, but the idea that this pass-time, this passion if you wish, could become a profession, didn't even cross his mind. It was necessary to work, and to work hard, to support the young family. When, in 1906, Vollard bought his whole studio from him, Maurice's father cried out, in a more astounded than questioning tone, "That stuff can really get sold?!" He really couldn't believe it!

Despite this first sale, this first success if you will, Vlaminck continued doing hard physical work. An exceptionally sturdy man, he knew how to make money, even by rowing. Already as an adult he had discovered in himself an incredible gift for the violin. His father was a music teacher. Every evening, he went down to Paris by train, even on foot when he didn't have a cent, to play in balls or theatres. This nocturnal occupation didn't bring in very much, but it had the advantage of leaving him free all day. To paint, of course.

I knew that as a young man he had been an extreme anarchist, but I didn't know that he had been initiated into this way of thinking during his time in the regiment, and that it was the army that familiarized him with the subversive ideas of the period. Conscripted in 1897, he was assigned to the regiment's band. That was normal for a musician. And the band left him with much leisure time. As incredible as it may appear, the library at the barracks was stocked with books by Marx, Zola and Kropotkine. Vlaminck devoured them literally. He even adhered to the revolutionary ideas to the point of becoming a member of a clandestine anarchist circle. Who knows where this could have led him, without his all-consuming passion for painting?

Few people know this story. I have it from the mouth of Vlaminck himself. Just like the story of his first meeting with Derain, which took place in a train, during a minor railway accident. André Derain was the son of a bourgeois family in Chatou. His parents intended him to pursue an engineering career that he refused outright. Forced to continue their journey on foot, young Maurice and André found themselves walking side by side after the accident. As they invariably got to talking, they discovered they shared a common passion for painting, and similar tastes in the field of artistic creation. By the end of their journey, they decided to work together. Which they did. After Vlaminck finished his military service, they set up their joint studio in a half-ruined restaurant on the Island of Chatou. They would paint for days on end, frenetically, using colours straight from their tubes, without mixing them. Their reds, yellows and blues rang out like explosions on the canvas. Fauvism was born.

The discovery of Van Gogh's paintings, exhibited in 1901 at Bernheim's, encouraged them to continue on their chosen path. But Vlaminck still waited until 1905 before starting to exhibit, or rather before taking part in exhibitions, such as the Salon of the Independent Artists, or the Autumn Salon where he even sold his first painting for one hundred francs, a derisory sum. It was there, also, that Vollard, the "new wave" art dealer, was so impressed on discovering him. One year later, he bought the whole collection of Vlaminck's studio, without knowing that this was a historical event, and a key moment in the history of art. A contract with Kahnweiler followed quite quickly, which led Vlaminck to think for the first time that he could make a living from his painting. Even if he didn't stop doing one night stands with his violin until 1910. As a bourgeois and much more sure of himself, Derain had already set himself up on rue Bonaparte.

But Vlaminck's joy was short-lived. The 1914-1917 war broke out, and with it the collapse of the art market. To feed his family, Maurice de Vlaminck was obliged to work in a factory. He did not go back to painting until around 1917. Today, it is difficult for us to imagine these lives "without a safety net." Lives of hard labour, deprivations and physical efforts. He had been living in La Tourillière only since 1925, with Berthe, his new wife, and his two daughters born from that union, and so Vlaminck hung onto that home, the way one can hang on to a refuge or a haven.

That man could do anything. He was gifted in everything, including writing. He even published several books, although his formal studies had been rather sketchy. These books were interesting and well written, even if Vlaminck had never considered himself as a writer. "I'm having fun," he said, "I'm neither accountable to anyone nor do I have to please anyone."

I was thinking of all that while seated opposite the great man, when a "eat, eat!" brought me back to reality. Vlaminck was the most charming of individuals, but he tended a bit to give orders. Scarcely had I emptied my plate when he again filled it with big chunks of meat. He had the appetite of an ogre. In his defense, I must admit that everything was delicious.

Coffee would be served in the studio, a large room behind the dining area. It was a bit atypical and strange as a place. Vlaminck had added it on to the house. On entering it, one was immediately struck by the view of the wheat fields that unfolded through the plate glass window. "All this is mine!", Maurice said, visibly proud of being a big property owner. The cups of coffee— and coffee was a big luxury--were accompanied by little glasses of alcohol as a "digestive." I don't know whether they really helped us digest, but we drank several of them because the food we had ingurgitated had been so heavy. Too heavy! I said to myself that the next time I would fast for a week before coming to the Vlamincks.

Maurice had his designated spot in a corner of the studio, where stood a brown, rather sunken armchair. When he settled himself in it, the springs flattened so much under his considerable weight, that one would have said he was seated on the ground. He would spend hours in this armchair: reading, writing, receiving visits. Books, manuscripts, scribbled sheets and pipes would pile up on a little table within easy reach of his hand. Photos of Van Dongen, Utrillo, and his daughters were tacked on the cabinet behind him. Former canvases, sculptures and African objects were lying around just about everywhere. A long time before, Vlaminck had discovered African art, unknown at the time in Europe, and had assembled over the years an attractive collection of it.

As Maurice had a Stentor-like voice, we all tended, when engaged in discussions with him, to raise our voices too. Conversations would then reach impressive, if not unimaginable decibel levels. Edwige, who had not inherited her father's voice, but his ability to cover up all the other voices, had an opinion on everything, even though she was only twenty-two years old, and spoke the whole time with a lighted cigarette in the corner of her mouth. She was truly her father's daughter. One realized immediately that she was the one who not only ran the house, but her father's farms and agricultural lands. Crazy about her Maurice to the point of worshipping him, Berthe was of a more unassuming, more discrete temperament. Having an oldest daughter so active and energetic suited him perfectly well. Of all the families of artists I knew, Vlaminck's was surely the most harmonious.

A bit of an actor, and a bit of a ham, Maurice liked to read out loud. As much as one could converse with him about this and that, interrupt him and contradict him, as much a dead silence would overcome the family assembly when he picked up a book. At that moment, he took his most recent, *Portrait avant décès* (A Portrait Before Death), and began reading for us a passage on the *Douanier Rousseau* (Rousseau the Customs Inspector). They had met at Vollard's in 1908. Then he happily read us a passage on Guillaume Apollinaire whom he had encountered at Madame de Kostrowitsky's, the latter's mother, in Chatou. After his readings, exciting I must say, we talked quite naturally about painting. Vlaminck never talked about his art, he knew his worth. Among the greatest. But he spoke willingly about others. Sometimes positively, sometimes negatively. His opinions were often cut-and-dried. But there was no one he detested and despised as much as Picasso. For Vlaminck, Picasso was the person responsible for the destruction of art. "He calculates, the little bastard, the cunning little devil," he said. Matisse did not please him either. "Look at Matisse's canvases," he said to me one day, "They are just interplays of colours. Change their places, reverse the green at the top and the pink at the bottom, it won't change anything. These are not canvases, they are shit!" Utrillo and the Naives found more favour in his eyes, whereas one would have thought the opposite.

After holding forth for a time, Maurice moved toward the little room at the back, the door of which was open. A room filled with paintings. "My latest canvases," Vlaminck said simply. Then he showed them to me one by one.

Without a word. Without a comment. In the most perfect of silences. But, behind this silence, one could distinctly hear the mute words: "All this is me!" Each time he showed me a painting, a landscape, flowers, or a seascape, he seemed to say: "And that, look, that is nothing, that?"

Soon I received a new invitation. Again "to chat." Vlaminck never wrote and never replied to letters. Yet many came to La Tourillière. He was inundated with mail. It was Bethe who took on the task of answering. And, by dint of doing it, she had acquired such skill in passing herself off as her husband—subjects, turns of phrases, style--that it was impossible to distinguish between the two of them. She even learned how to imitate his signature. To perfection!

Once again, I could not escape the traditional blowout. Except that this time, anticipating what would happen, I arrived on a completely empty stomach. First we ate partridges done in the Vlaminck way. A mountain of partridges! Seeing my astonishment over this quantity, he burst out laughing: "I don't have a rifle, I don't have bullets, and yet I don't lack for game, eh! And look at the roast beef that is coming! The whole of last week my wife wouldn't stop saying: 'Maurice, we have no more meat, Maurice, we have no more meat.' The idea of not having enough makes her a bit crazy, it anguishes her terribly. We didn't have any meat in the house, while having stables full of animals. It would have been a shame not to take advantage of it. So I sought out my farm boy, nearby. We chose a good animal, the kind that made it worth running the risk of landing in prison. I told the boy to prepare everything properly for the night, with the ax well sharpened, the knives too and the stall thoroughly cleaned. And also candles, many candles. Electricity could have drawn the attention of a neighbour or a passer-by. Everything went well, we worked hard, covered in blood, when suddenly the door opened and I heard Edwige's strident scream, surprised by all this blood. The poor girl was looking for me everywhere and couldn't find me. She didn't know that we were killing a cow on the quiet!"

The whole of France was being rationed, and Vlaminck was eating even better than before the war!

He enjoyed a great deal telling stories of ordinary life. And he did it so well, that they would become extraordinary. He had a real gift as a storyteller.

As the afternoon was radiant, we went outside to take a tour of his property. He probably didn't do it too often, because how else could one explain his surprise on coming upon a tent set up behind his house. He had never seen it before. It was Edwige's idea. She preferred to sleep under the tent because of the heat. Maurice thought the idea was so foolish that he called his daughter an imbecile. The discovery of this tent made him deeply pensive. He had seen a sign there. His daughter was probably not well. He asked me that very evening to welcome her in Paris, to take her out a bit, so that she would have a change of ideas. She enjoyed dancing.

Too young no doubt for so many responsibilities, Edwige was in charge of running La Tourillière night and day. She did it with a remarkable abnegation. Maurice told me that sending her to Paris for a week would be, in a way, a reward.

A few days later, I saw her come into my office, holding a little valise. To my work during the day was thus added an escort service in the evening. Or, rather, at night, since the evenings could be long.

THE RUDIERS

The Rudier Art Foundries [1] were located in Malakoff, at the entrance to Paris. The business which had to close after the war, after Eugène Rudier's death, was a remarkable institution, one–of–a kind, and enjoyed a world-wide reputation. The signature "Alexis Rudier, Foundry Artist, Paris," at the base of a bronze, was the guarantee of irreproachable quality. The most beautiful and perfect of qualities. The Rudiers were the ones who cast the works of Rodin, Bourdelle and Maillol.

In Malakoff, a large main entrance opened up onto a narrow, but deep courtyard. At the entrance, a modest office where the secretary worked; at the back, the foundries themselves. That courtyard was a veritable museum. Bronzes already cast waited there to be picked up by their owners. It was in the sun and under the rain that their patinas were completed. On arriving, I saw a *Penseur* (Thinker) by Rodin, and, further on, a *Bourgeois de Calais* (Burger of Calais), [2] *L'Ombre* [3] even further on, and, at the very back, *Les Trois Grâces* (The Three Graces) by Maillol. It was magical!

Before accessing the workshops, one passed through a vast hall where Rudier would stock his plasters and castings. There were many works by Rodin,

---

1. Founded by the three Rudier brothers, including Alexis, the business developed especially after the death of the latter. His son Eugène Rudier, who succeeded him, turned it into an art foundry with an international reputation. At the death of Eugène Rudier, in 1952, his widow carried out his final wishes. She had the moulds of the foundry destroyed, and she burned the archives, so that everything would stop and that no one could succeed her late husband. (EdN)

2 .A fragment of a famous ensemble by Rodin. (EdN)

3. A famous sculpture by Rodin, representing a man naked, standing up, with his head leaning heavily on his left shoulder. (EdN)

Maillol and nudes by Despiau. On the back wall one could see hanging the large semi-circular casting of the *Diane couchée avec le cerf* (Diana sleeping with the stag) by Benvenuto Cellini, the ancient founding of which is housed at the Louvre. The original, one can say, was cast in France because it had to serve as an impost at the chateau of Fontainebleau. Later on, Henri II offered it as a gift to Diane de Poitiers, to adorn the door of her chateau d'Anet. Happy to see me, since we were already friends, Rudier explained to me that this Diane was the first casting commissioned by the Germans. It was a special commission from Marshal Göring, intended to decorate his hunting castle of Carinhall. [4] What luck that he was content with a copy, I had thought. He could have easily confiscated the original from the Louvre! Goering had ordered a copy to be made of another Diane d'Anet, the one by Jean Goujon. Thinking he was a great connoisseur that he obviously was not, he ordered one of the dogs removed. This removal destroyed Goujon's marvelous composition. Shortly before the Allies landed, he had also commissioned a copy of the *Victoire de Samothrace* (The Victory of Samothrace). But since Paris was on the verge of falling, and the work on the copy was not completed, the unfinished work was shipped as is, to be finished in Germany. I had heard this story much later. It left me speechless.

In Rudier's large workshop, the plasters were set up on shelves, all along the walls. The middle of the room thus remained quite open. Here was where the workers brought or stored the bronzes already cast and polished, ready for the final touch, the patina.

In addition to the perfection of its castings, the foundry owed its reputation to the unbelievable quality of its patinas. Thanks to my friend Rudier's explanations, I learned everything about the processes that made possible the colours, shadows, brushstrokes, as well as the smoothing and shining done by hand.

There was in his place an extraordinary little Egyptian bronze cat, the perfect twin of the one at the Louvre, to the point that, if one had made an exchange, no one would have noticed it. Its pale green, mat patina was quite simply unique, inimitable. By way of an explanation, Rudier told me that he had bathed the cat in milk for months. And he was telling the truth! His experience with casting and patina was such, that he knew things that no one else knew.

---

4. Marshal Hermann Göring's country residence, situated in the middle of the Schorfheide forest, in the present state of Brandebourg. Built in 1933 in the style of hunting lodges, enlarged later on, it housed numerous works of art coming from occupied European countries. (EdN)

His golden bronzes were, they too, incomparable. He would cover the work with gold leaf, but in the end kept the gold only as a patina base. He would then reduce it so that only a luminous sheen would remain. The result was quite simply sublime.

Having one day received the order from Abetz to cast a copy of the equestrian statue of Charlemagne, the one at the Carnavalet Museum, [5] for the chancellery in Berlin, Rudier discovered that this rather tarnished little masterpiece had certainly been gilded when created. And he ascertained this even though the work had deteriorated to the point that one could no longer see any trace of this gold. Instead of wearing himself out trying to gild its copy, which would risk turning it into a kitsch object, he remade it exactly identical to the original one, as it was in 1940. It was extraordinary! He had found the way of giving something new to the patina and the blemishing effect of time.

The large buildings on the right-hand side of the courtyard housed the foundry itself. Rudier fashioned all of his castings with sand, and not wax, like the near-totality of his colleagues. This technique, very difficult to master, made the extremely striking fineness of his realizations possible. I had the opportunity to convince myself of it, since I had the immense privilege to witness the casting of Rodin's *Porte de l'enfer* (The Gate of Hell). [6] In 1880, the Rudier foundry had realized the very first commission of this masterpiece, earmarked for the Musée des arts décoratifs (The Museum of Decorative Arts). Rodin had such confidence in the quality of their work that once the plaster version left his studio on the rue de l'Université, he didn't concern himself about it anymore. This blind confidence of his was such that Rodin had never set foot in Rudier's ateliers. He thought that his foundry expert was far more competent that he was himself to carry out the work perfectly. Besides, later on, Rudier became the official foundry expert for the Musée Rodin (The Rodin Museum). [7]

Rodin had some hare-brained ideas that were entirely his own. Thus, he strongly insisted that his bronzes be absolutely identical to their plaster ver-

---

5. A statuette that came from the treasure-house of the Metz cathedral. Sold several times during the 19th century, it was bought by the City of Paris, and stored at the Carnavalet Museum, then at the Louvre. (EdN)

6. The author does not say this, but it was a commission from Arno Breker, the official sculptor of the Third Reich. (EdN)

7. After the death of Auguste Rodin, in 1917, Eugène Rudier obtained the exclusive rights to the castings for the Musée Rodin. (EdN)

sions. Even if the plaster versions had flaws. Rudier related to me that the clay form of *Éve* (Eve) [8] was held up thanks to a strong iron framework. When the plaster poured, it was noticed that the iron bar was sticking out of the right leg. But Rodin, for reasons that no one could explain, refused to touch it. And one can still see it, today, sticking out of the bronze.

"Ah, he had his ideas!"

That was one of Rudier's favourite expressions, a man who was not all that talkative. Except that he liked to tell stories. For example, the one about *l'Homme au nez cassé* (The Man With The Broken Nose). [9] Just as work on the clay was finished, the head fell and the nose was damaged in the fall as it hit the edge of a stool. Rodin didn't want to touch it again. "Out of superstition," Rudier told me. When the art work was exhibited, critics and enthusiastic art fans saw in it a portrait of Michelangelo.

All of Rudier's plaster workers were Italians. According to him, the Italians were particularly skillful for this fine and delicate job.

Rudier did not only work in bronze, he was also very impressive with lead, a more tender and difficult material to manipulate. Maillol often commissioned him to do castings in lead. He found that these were very well–suited to the round shapes of his women and that time had a wonderful effect on the material's colour. Rudier had acquired such a mastery in this field that he was the one who received the enormous commission for Versailles before the war. All the statues surrounding the basins in the park, as well as the decorations on the rooftops, were in lead. And since time had gnawed at this beautiful but soft material, it would be necessary to redo and consolidate everything. The hardest part, said Rudier, was getting these enormous objects out of the basins, and removing them from their location. In any event, all of the statues of Versailles had passed through his foundry. The man was very agreeable, very friendly, and his place was magical for any person sensitive to beauty and to the products of art.

I visited Rudier because, in spite of the restrictions, he had received a very important commission from the German government. It was to cast all of Arno Breker's bronze statues, which would be exhibited at the Orangerie during

---

8. A work intended at the outset as part of the Porte de l'enfer, but unfinished because the model, who was pregnant, could no longer pose as Eve. Auguste Rodin would exhibit it later, as it was. (EdN)

9. Portrait of a labourer in the Saint-Marcel neighbourhood, known by the name of Bibi. (EdN)

his big exhibition, or rather the big retrospective of his whole work. [10] It was Albert Speer, [11] a close friend of Breker, who made sure that Rudier received the metals necessary for the realization of these often imposing works by the principal artist of the Reich.

Next to the foundry, a little house filled with extraordinary art works, and surrounded by a beautiful rose garden, served as a place to welcome important clients who wished to spend several days there. But, because of the war, of the Occupation and gasoline rationings, Rudier had transformed it into a dwelling for his wife and himself. Because they would no longer make the accustomed round-trips between Paris and Le Vésinet, where they had a very attractive property. In my time, they would go there only on Sundays. I know, because they often invited me to accompany them, which I did with pleasure.

The Rudier's rich property enclosed a lovely park with ponds, a marvellous spot! The house was filled with masterpieces. There were sculptures everywhere. Even in the park, under the large trees. On the street side, stood *L'Ombre* by Rodin,[12] a sculpture two metres high, destined to adorn Rudier's tomb. This sinister foresight astonished me a bit, because Rudier was in excellent shape. Opposite the house, he had acquired a large wooded area, where one could see the *Trois Grâces* by Maillol, works by Bourdelle, other Rodins; the *Faune* (The Faun) by Dardé, [13] cast in lead, three metres high, flashed a diabolical smile between the trees.

Behind the park, there was a little villa, the former property of Rudier's wife, where the couple had settled a gravely ill Antoine Bourdelle, and who died there. After his death, they had sold it to Lucie Valore, [14] the year of her

---

10. The exhibition took place in 1942. (EdN)

11. A German architect, the principal architect of the Nazi Party, of which he had been a member since 1931. The Minister of Armaments and War Production within the Third Reich. He was judged and condemned during the Nuremberg Trials. He was the author of the best-seller *In the Heart of the Third Reich*, published in Germany in 1969, then in the whole world. And which led to an American television series. (EdN)

12. A work representing Adam intended originally as part of *La porte de l'enfer*, but finally exhibited alone, like Eve. Like Eve, Adam is unfinished, he doesn't have a hand. This sculpture adorns, in fact, the tomb of Eugène Rudier, in the cemetery of Le Vésinet.

13. *Faune poursuivant une nymphe* (Faun Pursuing a Nymph) by Paul Dardé (1888-1963), a French sculptor, who formerly worked for Rodin. (EdN)

14. French artist and painter, born Lucile Veau, the widow of a rich Belgian banker and collector of Utrillo's paintings, Robert Pauwels. Encouraged by Suzanne Valadon, Lucie married Suzanne's son, Maurice Utrillo, in 1935. (EdN)

marriage to Maurice Utrillo.

Although we were on very friendly terms, Rudier and I still did not see each other all the time, and especially not during his working hours. You can thus imagine my surprise when I saw him one morning as I was coming to my office, walking back and forth on the sidewalk in front of 52 avenue des Champs-Élysées. In general, he always had his secretary inform me of his visits. Or he would call on me unexpectedly at noon, to take me with him for an aperitif at his friend Francis' place, who ran a luxury-style grocery store at the corner of the avenue Montaigne and the rue Bayard. His Bar américain (American Bar) has since been replaced by the Dior boutique.

Conscious of my questioning glance, Rudier began by telling me that his nephew Georges, whom I did not know, had set up at Montrouge a small industrial foundry, specializing in spare parts for the railways. Now, they were without any news from Georges, because Georges had been taken to the rue des Saussaies [15] by the German police. I had no other choice but to betake myself to the Gestapo, a route with which I was familiar ever since the problem I had to resolve concerning Dina Vierny, Maillol's model, which I will relate later. I must say that the officers of the German police were rather affable as they explained to me that Georges Rudier was involved in an affair of metal trafficking. Nothing political, then. Whew! I was afraid he might be a resistant, or something like that. Since he wasn't, I was lucky to be able to get him out of there.

Nevertheless, I had to negotiate for a long time before convincing them that this was not dramatic, that it was not necessary to make a big fuss about the affair. I had trouble succeeding, because metal was a strategic material during the war. It was thus rather grave. Obviously, I didn't neglect to let slip that the uncle of the man taken in for questioning was the foundry artist for Arno Breker, and, as such, "a close friend of Germany." Finally, they agreed to free him, but on the strict condition that he close his shop. Because, if he continued, he would need metals, and would thus find it necessary to resume trafficking. How could they be sure he would close his shop? Seeing the problem, I then proposed to them that Georges be placed under the guardianship of his uncle, a man worthy of confidence and a "great friend of the Reich." My proposal was

---

15. Between 1940 and 1944 at 11 rue des Saussaies, stood the headquarters of the German Police for Security Investigation, including Section IV, known by the name of the Gestapo. Today, the building is occupied by the General Administration of the National Police, as well as by the General Administration of the National Gendarmerie. (EdN)

accepted and I left the Gestapo office with young Rudier, pale but happy. He had escaped by the skin of his teeth. They would have shipped him to Germany. It was a foregone conclusion.

Having neither a personal vehicle nor one that went with my job, I would do my errands on foot or by subway. Except when Rudier came to pick me up, which happened quite often. Like Vlaminck, he loved the big powerful cars. Three beautiful American cars were on blocks in the former stables of his home in Le Vésinet. He could not use them because of the restrictions. Compelled to find other means of transportation, he had hitched a handsome horse named Ripp to a little English car. So one could see him getting around in the streets of Paris, at the wheel of a two-seater vehicle, drawn by a horse. It was funny, of course, but slow, very slow. Consequently he bought himself an old Citroën, converted to gaz. The French were forbidden from driving with gasoline. But since one could find gasoline on the black market, and since Rudier was not exactly short of money, his car was always filled to the top. The very visible bottle of gaz, in the back of the car, was there simply to avoid police inspections. In the event that he would be inspected, which never happened, Rudier had installed a little tap close at hand, that would cut the flow of gasoline and make the car switch over to gaz.

During his sojourn in Paris in 1943, which I will talk about further on, Maillol had also profited greatly from Rudier's car.

KIND LUCIE

Mme Utrillo would come to see me so often that I ended up wondering whether she didn't have a soft spot for me. I was only thirty, whereas she... She would reproach me for not coming to visit them, she and Utrillo, when I would go to the Rudier's home, at Le Vésinet. It's true that I would go there often.

So one Sunday, I covered the several metres that separated the Rudiers' property from the Utrillos', where at the entrance I saw a disarming inscription: "La Bonne Lucie" (Kind Lucie). She received me very graciously, but locked the door behind her on leaving. So what people were saying was true: Maurice Utrillo was literally locked up in his own home, in order not to escape his wife's finicky vigilance. Lucie proudly showed me her garden, of which all the trees had been cut down in favour of a carefully tended lawn surrounded by stone arcades. There was also a large aviary filled with exotic birds. Everything there was rather ill-assorted, including the house which had a vague "Swiss chalet" look about it. Along the whole length of the facade, strangely whitewashed, Lucie had a terrace constructed, adorned at either end by a huge glass ball. These strange balls could be illuminated in different colours, according to Madame's mood: red, yellow or blue. Lucie was very proud of this invention.

Inside, everything was white and gold. Dazzling, scintillating, and monotonous. Even the piano was in white and gold! Fortunately, on the wall there were paintings by Maurice of some of the famous streets in Montmartre.. They broke up this monotony. Utrillo was delighted to see me. Enclosed as he was, the poor man saw few people. Exceptionally, he was allowed a little glass of red wine. His studio was on the upper floor, at the end of a narrow staircase:

a little room with an easel in the middle. And in front of the easel, a chair. It was in this monastic ambiance that he created his paintings that gave so much pleasure to French and foreigners alike.

He was in the process of working on a view of the Sacré-Coeur under the snow. And placed next to it, the same subject in the summer. Lucie had pinned up a bit of cardboard on which she had written, in large letters, the word: "Snow!" So Utrillo had to redo the same subject under the snow. That was an order.

Critics often bore down on Utrillo, because he worked too often from post-cards and not enough from nature. That was very unfair! Utrillo managed to recreate nature from postcards, whereas many others could only make post-cards when painting nature. He was a modest genius and, truly, a very touching man.

Behind the house where they lived, there was a funny little shed. A chapel, really, where Utrillo would go to meditate at length every Friday, the day on which Joan of Arc died.

Before her marriage, "Kind Lucie" had tried her hand at literature, even at drama. She produced plays that others wrote, but which she signed under the name of Pauwels. It was one failure after another. It reached a point where these flops were beginning to cost a lot, even if she had money. Her marriage to Utrillo was an affair of epic proportions, because it took place completely without the main party being involved. Lucie negotiated the marriage contract with Suzanne Valadon, Maurice's mother. The poor man tried to escape from the whole business till the very end, but in vain, and including in the church, during the marriage ceremony.

Once married, Lucie had two goals. The first: making her husband work. And the second: preventing him from drinking. Lost far from Montmartre, poor Utrillo didn't even have the right to enter the bistros in Le Vésinet. He had to paint, paint and paint some more. Lucie took care of everything else. She would sign the contracts with the dealers and she was in charge of the publicity. Until the day when she discovered that she, too, had a gift. Lucie absolutely wanted to show me her still lifes, her flowers and, especially, her portrait of Maurice. A beautiful portrait, except that one felt the master had helped her a bit. A bit and probably a lot. I learned later on that Lucie obliged Utrillo's dealer to buy one of her own canvases, every time he purchased one by Maurice. "Kind Lucy" was a redoubtable woman!

In the evening, at dinner, the Rudiers related to me a very funny incident that had occurred the preceding week. Mme Utrillo was crying at the butcher's in Le Vésinet to get a roast of beef. He refused to yield. It was the period of ration coupons. To obtain a piece of meat was no small matter. In desperation, Lucie offered the butcher a painting by Utrillo. Obviously, the butcher immediately cut off a splendid roast of beef for her. Except that, the following day, she brought him a picture painted by herself, and signed "Fernande Alexandrine.

When I returned to Paris, in 1950, I met Lucie by chance at Paul Pétridès, on rue La Boétie. She had doubled in size. Her face was smeared with a thick coating of foundation cream and the flowery hat she wore was also two times bigger than before. As for the rows of pearls around her thick neck, they had tripled.

By way of a reply to my friendly greeting, she called out, almost disappointed to see me: "But they told me that you were dead!"

Having said that, "Kind Lucie" hastened to show me proudly her decoration as a Resistance fighter. I still wonder whom she could have really resisted. Certainly not poor Maurice.

GEORGES MARATIER

Georges Maratier [1] was among the very first to come and see me at the Champs-Élysées. We had met before the war. Since I hadn't had the time to inform him about it, he did not know that I was in Paris, but he thought he recognized my signature at the bottom of a German document authorizing the opening of an exhibition, and he came to ascertain this with his own eyes.

We had befriended one another in 1938. I was in Paris to visit a certain number of exhibitions that Berlin was talking about. During my peregrinations I found myself at the corner of the rue de Lille and the rue de Beaune where the poster "Guillaume Apollinaire and His Painters" caught my eye. Paintings and documents concerning the poet filled all the halls of the gallery. Seeing that I was so visibly interested, the master of the place came over to me. It was Georges Maratier, an impassioned lover of the art at the beginning of the century, [2] and a true friend of Apollinaire even though he had made the poet's acquaintance a very short time before the latter's death. They had met on November 11, 1918, the day France was celebrating the Armistice, at a moment when the poet was dying in a little apartment. [3] Already drained physically as a result of war wounds, Apollinaire had caught the Spanish grippe that was then raging in Paris. Too weakened, he died of it. After his death, Maratier remained very close to Jacqueline, his widow. Maratier supported her as much as he could, including financially. Although she no longer lived in Paris, she

---

1. A businessman, art dealer, director of an art gallery, friend and confident of Gertrude Stein. (EdN)

2. The author is referring to the beginning of the 20th century. (EdN)

3. At 202 boulevard Saint-Germain. (EdN)

had done everything to ensure that Apollinaire's apartment would remain as it had been at the moment of his death, its walls covered with canvases by the Douanier Rousseau, Picasso, the great cubists, and with paintings by Marie Laurencin. Even the helmet pierced by the bullet that wounded the poet so very seriously was there. Jacqueline had never given thought to sell the least important of these paintings, which, nonetheless, were already worth a great deal of money. Everything was extraordinary in this story.

A gravely wounded war veteran, Guillaume had met Jacqueline in the hospitals of Paris where he was being treated. Consequently, she was his nurse before becoming his wife, a very beautiful, generous and charitable wife. They got married in 1918, a few months before Apollinaire's death. And their marriage witnesses were Picasso and Vollard.

Jacqueline had helped Maratier considerably in the preparation of this exhibition. She was the one who had provided the major portion of the works exhibited and the whole body of letters. The large painting by Marie Laurencin that had pride of place in the middle of the exhibition also belonged to Jacqueline. It dated from the period when Marie and Guillaume were lovers. "Apollinaire and His Friends" showed Guillaume in top shape, surrounded by his pals Picasso, Fernande Olivier and Jacqueline herself, a true guardian of the temple.

Maratier had all the details of Apollinaire's life at his fingertips. One would have said that not one anecdote had escaped him. He often met Angelica de Kostrowitzky, a beautiful Polish aristocrat, the mother of two boys born from unknown fathers, one of whom was Guillaume. Born in Rome, Apollinaire had spent his childhood in the south of France and did not come to Paris until he was twenty. Stateless, poor, without any relations, he went through hard times. Through a fortunate combination of circumstances he became the tutor to the children of a rich German woman, and fell madly in love with their beautiful governess. This passionate love inspired him to write his first poems, published in *La Revue Blanche* (The White Review). In that period, too, he met his two best friends: Pablo Picasso and Max Jacob, as well as Marie Laurencin to whom Picasso introduced him. Instantaneous love at first sight. Those two were so beautiful and in love that they inspired the Douanier Rousseau, another close friend of Apollinaire, to do his painting *La Muse inspirant le poète* (The Muse Inspiring the Poet). It was to honour Rousseau, on the occasion of the presentation of this painting at the Salon des Indépendants, that Apollinaire organized at the Bateau-Lavoir, in Picasso's studio, the famous banquet that was an event in art history.

It was Maratier who informed me of something I did not know, namely, that Apollinaire had gone to prison for the theft of a painting at the Louvre. A theft of which, finally, he was not guilty. And also that he had wanted to commit suicide when Marie Laurencin left him for someone else.

I learned all that in 1938. In 1940, things had changed to such an extent that Maratier was preparing to close his gallery. Georges was not one of these typical gallery owners, I must say, whose universe is limited to paintings that they sell or to the money they either get or don't get. He was interested in literature, dance, music, and theatre. He had founded the Éditions de la Montagne, produced plays and collaborated with Serge Diaghilev's Ballets Russes.

It was in his gallery one day that I met Wilhelm Uhde, a German art lover and collector who had been residing in France since the beginning of the century and was the owner of a small gallery. It was said that he had been the "discoverer" of the Douanier Rousseau, and he really had been. As a lover of the kind of painting that others considered as "naive," he had been particularly involved with a group of artists called "peintres du dimanche" (Spare Time Painters), including Bauchant, Vivin and Séraphine, his former cleaning lady in Senlis. He called them "painters of the sacred heart." Thanks to him, they occupy today their rightful place, and what a place, in the greatest museums. The exhibition "Apollinaire and His Painters" reminded him of that whole period, when those artists would get together at Gertrude Stein's. Since I did not know her, Uhde strongly insisted that Maratier introduce us.

GERTRUDE STEIN

Two days later, we were off to visit Gertrude Stein. Since I didn't really know who she was, Maratier explained to me, on our way there, that although an American, she was the heiress of Jewish bankers from Vienna. Not as rich as when her father was alive, she still had, he told me, considerable financial assets. Gertrude and her younger brother Leo, Maratier informed me, had left America for love of French painting, especially of Gauguin and Cézanne. Rich and crazy, they supposedly took up residence in Paris because in Florence, a lover of Cézanne's art had recommended to them a small Parisian gallery, on rue Lafitte, telling them that they would find the most beautiful Cézannes there. It was, quite obviously, Vollard's gallery.

According to Maratier, a bit jealous no doubt, Vollard and the Steins could not help but get along well. First of all, because, like them, he came from far, from the Île de la Réunion. Secondly, because, like them, he was whimsical, eccentric and wild: at a time when he was already an important art dealer, he would stock in his reserves hundreds of canvases by Gauguin, Cézanne, Renoir, Picasso, Braque, Derain, Vlaminck, without selling them, without even exhibiting them. During the Steins first visit at Vollard's, even when they had told him right off the bat why they had come there, Vollard kept them dangling for hours, without showing them the slightest canvas. It was only at the very end of the evening, when he saw they were exhausted, that he brought down from the first floor a little Cézanne landscape which the Steins bought without thinking, almost without looking at it. At least, that is what Maratier had told me. Beautiful stories are true, or become true with time. Be that as it may, Vollard and the Steins became great friends, and Vollard earned a lot of money thanks to the rich Gertrude.

We had almost reached rue Christine, where Gertrude Stein was living in 1938, but Maratier told me that the mythical address on rue Fleurus would forever remain her home. A studio had been added to that apartment. Empty at first, its walls were destined to receive the future collection. One of the first paintings they hung up was *Une fille nue avec un panier de fleurs* (Naked Girl with a Flower Basket). Sagot, the little art dealer who had sold it to them, told them that the young painter had barely arrived from Spain. Obviously, he referred to Pablo Picasso who would rapidly become one of the habitués of the rue Fleurus. Today everybody knows the *Portrait de Gertrude Stein* (Portrait of Gertrude Stein). [1] But few people know that the rich American woman had moved up for months to Montmartre to pose at the Bateau-Lavoir. After 90 sessions, the painting was still not finished! Picasso couldn't do it. To extricate himself, he completely erased Gertrude's head and repainted it from memory. It was not really a good likeness of her. I have always enjoyed these stories of painters and their masterpieces. True or false, what difference does it make? When I was a student, I adored the story of Michelangelo painting the Sistine Chapel while Pope Julius II was howling, crazed with rage. According to the legend, Michelangelo had painted a masterpiece even though he wasn't even a "real" painter!

The more Maratier was talking to me about Gertrude Stein, the more impatient I was to get to her place. I was impatient to see the paintings of her collection, all those masterpieces. It was also on rue Fleurus, Maratier told me, that Gertrude Stein became a great writer. I would read her *Three Lives and The Making of Americans* much later. Two very beautiful books, indeed.

An elderly lady had opened the door for us on rue Christine. She was Gertrude Stein's faithful secretary and friend, Alice Toklas, a thin little woman. She and Maratier knew one another well, visibly, since they started chatting as though they were picking up a conversation begun the day before. They talked about cooking: good recipes, good dishes, good wines. The kinds of things that I, a little German guy, knew nothing about. The face of Alice Toklas, with her aquiline nose, was strange. But even stranger was her grating, rusty voice, and her dreadful Anglo-French jargon. It was interminable, but there was nothing I could do. So only after they had finished chatting did we proceed to the living room where Gertrude Stein was seated.

Even today, I remember this vision very well. Unforgettable! She was very

---

1. A canvas by Pablo Picasso, painted in 1906. (EdN)

imposing, but I would not say that she was really fat. Moreover, I wonder whether her way of dressing did not accentuate this impressive aspect of her physique. She had very large shoulders and a majestic head with a crown-like halo of grey hair, arranged somewhat in the style of the Roman emperors, which gave Gertrude Stein the aura of a historical monument.

There were paintings everywhere. Many cubists. Pictures by Juan Gris and Picasso. Her large portrait by Picasso dominated the room. This painting, reproduced everywhere, and which can be found at the Metropolitan in New York, I saw it myself at Gertrude Stein's and in her presence. Having learned about her life only a little while before, and seeing the model and the painting thirty years later, I thought that Gertrude Stein had ended up resembling her unfaithful portrait painted by Picasso. There was something magical about the whole thing.

When I introduced myself, I had pronounced my name in the French way. Lange became, in French, l'Ange (The Angel).

"Oh, the blue angel," Gertrude Stein said, smiling. "Marlene..."

The conversation could have been painful. After all, I came from Nazi Germany, from "the Germany of Hitler" as one would say in that period, but thanks to this little allusion to Marlene Dietrich, she was lively and friendly. We were among connoisseurs, among art lovers. The rest didn't count.

While we were talking, Alice set up a little table covered by a tablecloth embroidered by her, and adorned with Gertrude Stein's amusing motto: "A rose is a rose is a rose is a rose." It was also inscribed on her stationery. The pastries, too, were made by Alice's white hands.

Obviously we spoke about Germany. At first a little, then we talked about nothing else. Gertrude seemed very worried and asked me a thousand questions. Without asking me, though, whether I was a Nazi myself. I was not, but I was German and I lived and worked in Germany. The new regime did not please her, she did not understand it. She did not bring up the "Jewish question" at all, but wanted rather to know everything about the Nazi policy in the domain of fine arts. Gertrude did not understand the concept "degenerate art" and wanted me to explain it to her. I did my best, but I doubt whether I succeeded.

At the moment when we took our leave, Gertrude Stein asked me insistently to come back and see her before I returned to Berlin. The times were turbulent, difficult, we were in September 1938, just after the Munich agreement.

When I returned to her place, I found her pensive, disquieted, worried by the political situation. For example, she told me that she didn't believe that the agreement signed in Munich would protect France from war. "The situation will be reversed," she said. I remember it very well.

As we said goodbye, she placed in my hands a little package, carefully wrapped, and said: "A souvenir from me." She didn't want me to open it right away. It was a very beautiful paper collage, slightly embossed, representing roses in a vase with her motto wrapped around it, *"A rose is a rose is a rose is a rose,"* Gertrude's symbol, followed by the large initials "G.S." and "A.T." written smaller. The whole gift was framed by lacy gold paper. Very beautiful and very touching! It goes without saying that I brought back this precious gift to Berlin. Mobilized because the war had begun, I entrusted it to the care of my mother, who had retired to the countryside.

In 1940, Gertrude Stein was obviously no longer in Paris. Maratier, who remained in contact with her, told me that she had withdrawn to the Free Zone.[2] Before she left, she had entrusted to him the safekeeping of her home on the rue Christine. He carried out this responsibility very well.

---

2. Gertrude Stein would die in 1946, at the American Hospital in Neuilly, at the age of 72. Having taken refuge in the Free Zone, she offered her services to translate Marshal Pétain's speeches in English. Protected during the war by Baron Dallemagne and Baroness Pierlot, her friend, Gertrude Stein met at the latter's home the poet and dramatist Paul Claudel. (EdN)

PLACE VENDÔME AND THE THÉÂTRE DES CHAMPS-ÉLYSÉES

A few days after my friend Maratier's surprise visit, I went to see him in his new gallery, on the Place Vendôme. He had set himself up there a little while before, after his return from the war where he had been a nurse. The debacle had brought him down to Arles.

He was now established at number 17, [1] right next to the Ritz. Associated with a certain René Drouin, Maratier remained the heart and soul of this gallery. Very well-connected and very competent, Georges organized important exhibitions, like, for example, the one devoted to Antoine Bourdelle, inaugurated by Louis Hautecoeur, [2] and the inaugural speech of which was pronounced by Maurice Denis, an old Nabi painter who had become a member of the Institut.

I can't resist quoting a small portion of the speech, because it is so steeped in the themes and style of the period. Here, then, is what Maurice Denis said when presenting the work of his friend Antoine Bourdelle:

"It is our old Gallo-Roman and Christian heritage, it is the spirit of the Occident that lives again in Bourdelle's mythologies. Whereas the Greeks aspire towards a kind of canonic perfection in which their decadence enclosed itself and grew weaker, he escapes from rules, he moves the axes elsewhere. He

---

1. At 17 Place Vendôme stands the Hôtel Crozat, one of the most ancient on the square, since it goes back to 1703. For a long time the property of the Crédit foncier de France, it was acquired by the Ritz in 1998. (EdN)

2. An art historian and high ranking civil servant, Curator of the Musée du Luxembourg and one of the founders of the Musée d'art moderne du Palais de Tokyo, Commander of the Légion d'honneur, General Manager of Fine Arts for the Government of Vichy, a position from which he would be removed on the order of Hermann Göring "for permanently refusing to collaborate." (EdN)

underlines the unexpected. He is an impressionist. He obeys only the logic of his craft and the sharpness of his sensations."

Maratier's gallery was big and beautiful, composed of several halls fitted with large panoramic windows that overlooked the Ritz' little garden where German generals liked to have their coffee. So one could see them strolling about, in twos or threes, with a cup in their hands, discussing important things, surely, but being oh so vulnerable. Once, in a joking tone, I told Maratier that his gallery was perfectly situated to commit terrorist attacks against top German officers. Although it was difficult to approach them in ordinary times, here they were offered on a platter, since one was literally a few metres from them. "Unimaginable," he whispered, visibly annoyed by my joke. Whereas on the contrary, it was perfectly imaginable.

One day when I was hanging about at Maratier's, I made the acquaintance of Edwin Livengood,[3] an American. An odd character, who spoke French with an accent you could cut with a knife. Having come to Paris a long time before to become a painter, Livengood quickly realized that he lacked talent, and became a bit like Maratier's shadow. The latter had not only introduced him into the milieu, but taught him the art dealer's trade.

I also met at Georges Maratier's an important Belgian man named Van den Klip, who had become very rich in the jute business. I knew nothing about it, but if I had understood correctly, he was henceforth involved in investing his money, a field in which he was also very skillful, according to what I had been told. Appreciating art, like many Belgians, Van den Klip succeeded in putting together an attractive collection which, every year, increased in value. A very cunning man, Livengood had not only managed to sell him paintings galore, but also to marry his daughter Chrystelle. A very charming lady by the way. With the financial help of his father-in-law, Livengood was able to open a lovely gallery on the rue des Beaux-Arts. In 1941, poor Edwin was, obviously, interned in a camp near Compiègne. Without being in the least anti-German, he still remained an American citizen. Now, on September 11, 1941, Germany declared war on the United States and all the Americans in the whole of France found themselves in jail. So once again, here I was on my way to the Hôtel Majestic, the headquarters of the Paris Military Command. Whereas I had a certain experience and, as a result, a certain know-how for liberating French people, Livengood was an American. This was different, and I really didn't

3. An art dealer, Edwin Livengood was already Georges Maratier's business partner during the 1930s, notably in the famous Galerie de Beaune. (EdN)

know how to go about it. I managed to anyway.

Maratier, who liked Livengood a lot, was delighted by this happy conclusion. I know, people find it hard to imagine, decades after the war, that things would unfold so easily, that the Germans would liberate prisoners at the request of a young officer of my rank. But that is what happened, I'm not making it up. I'm simply relating what I lived, saw and heard. Happy, then, Maratier dragged me out of his gallery to show me a beautiful mansion, again on Place Vendôme, next to Van Cleef and Arpels. [4] He was negotiating with someone or other, to open a big gallery there on several floors. The beautiful building was entirely empty, if not abandoned. One gained entrance to it through a large main door that opened up on a courtyard paved with marble. The facade adorned with four Corinthian columns must have dated from Louis XV. A very classy staircase led from the ground floor to the vestibule on the first which gave access to large halls perfect for exhibiting paintings. I could really not find any reasons why the German authorities would be against this initiative, so I congratulated my friend on this beautiful discovery. That is how Georges Maratier went from number 17 to number 20 on the Place Vendôme. And his first exhibition in the new premises was devoted to Edouard Vuillard, who had passed away at La Baule in 1940.

Maratier and Vuillard were very close. His best friend and army comrade Jacques Roussel, was none other than the son of the painter K.X. Roussel, a friend of Vuillard since childhood, because they had been schoolmates at the Lycée Condorcet. Roussel was the one who could persuade Vuillard, almost against his will, to enter the Paris Académie des beaux-arts (School of Fine Arts). Both were admitted with flying colours, but nevertheless left the noble institution which they found dusty, for the Académie Julian, where they met--I have already said it, I think, but it is not useless to repeat it--Bonard, Maurice Denis and Vallotton. They would become the Nabis, as we know, under the influence of Gauguin. But the ties between Vuillard and Roussel would grow even stronger when the former married Marie, the sister of the latter. Georges Maratier's best friend was, thus quite simply, Vuillard's nephew. When Vuillard, who had no children, died, all his estate went to his beloved sister, and consequently to the Roussels, whose family in the meantime had become bigger. Appointed as the expert to distribute the inheritance equitably, Maratier had done his job very well. He would do it again at the death of K.X. Roussel

---

4. A famous jewelry store which is still on the Place Vendôme. (EdN)

in 1944.

Despite the war, the Occupation and the shortages, the magnificent Vuillard exhibition was a resounding success. It must be said that Maratier outdid himself. The mounting was magnificent, and the works were presented in a sumptuous manner.

Strengthened by this enormous success, Maratier did it again with another no less grandiose exhibition devoted to K.X. Roussel, already an elderly gentleman at 78 years old. Evidently, it was out of the question to admit the public without the approval of the master who was invited two or three days before the opening, when all the canvases were already hung up.

It was a courtesy visit, which would not have had any consequences if suddenly the old Roussel hadn't noticed that all the works were not signed. There was a large outburst of laughter! What to do? The master was far too elderly to climb up a ladder, with his paintbrush in hand.

"Jacques," Roussel said suddenly to his son, "You will have a signature contest with Georges. The one who wins, will have the privilege of signing my paintings."

No sooner said than done. Under our mesmerized gaze, the gallery owner and the artist's son practiced for a while on a slip of paper, with the master looking on approvingly. Maratier won the contest, and so had the honour of putting the signature "K.X. Roussel" at the bottom of a certain number of paintings, thereby turning them instantaneously into fakes.

Few people are aware of this curious session. I can see from here the experts examining the signature with a magnifying glass, to determine if they are really in the body of the work. Since then, these Roussels signed by Maratier have been circulating. A certain number of them can even be found in the national museums.

One day, rather astonished, I was informed by the receptionist that Georges Maratier was at the *Propagandastaffel*, but not to see me. Scarcely did I have the time to be astonished by it than Georges was already pushing my office door open. Visibly moved, he told me that the directorship of the Théâtre des Champs-Élysées was vacant, and that he wanted it. Georges had always dreamed of being a theatre director, and thought that the time was ripe. Besides, he was in our offices to talk about it with Lieutenant Frank, my counterpart for the theatre. Since the German authorities had requisitioned the Théâtre des Champs-Élysées, its administration was entirely in the hands of Frank. Maratier had thus gone knocking at the right door. Except that being an aggressive, complex-ridden person, full of contradictions, Frank replied with one word: "Nein!"

I explained to Maratier that in civil life, Frank was a lackluster man, without any stature, that he suffered from multiple inhibitions, including an inferiority complex. Hence his brusqueness, sister of brutality. A narrow-minded Nazi, he viewed himself, out of sheer ignorance, as the king of Parisian theatre.

Maratier should have come and seen me first. But what was done was done. Now it would be necessary to remain patient.

I let a few days pass, but not more than a week, before sounding out Frank. Not in his office, where he was domineering and sure of himself. I approached him at the canteen, at lunchtime. As though nothing had happened, I asked him between two mouthfuls, what he had against the art dealer. However ignorant Frank may have been, he wasn't an idiot. So he understood right away what I was getting at.

"Let them take charge of painting and not the theatre!" He answered me dryly.

I tried to explain to him that painting and drama had points in common. I launched into convolutions that I myself had sometimes trouble following. With the help of Calvados, Frank was listening to me in a more and more relaxed manner. As a result, our conversation went on until the end of the meal. Since it would soon be necessary to return to work, I asked him what saying "no" to Maratier would bring him. He thought about it for a few seconds before answering, in his habitual style: "Nothing! You're bugging me..."

"Say 'yes' to him," I retorted, "and I won't bug you anymore."

"I like you, Lange," he answered me, smiling. "But you are impossible with your French! Alright, agreed, to your health nonetheless!"

We drank our glasses of Calvados bottoms up, which meant clearly that our agreement was sealed.

I went over to Place Vendôme to convey the good news. Maratier didn't want to believe me. He was mad with joy!

The speech with which I had knocked Frank out senseless was certainly hazy, in part at least, but there was still an element of truth in it. At least as concerned the Théâtre des Champs-Élysées. Quite simply because this Mecca of drama and music had been built, decorated, and nourrished by a series of very great artists. Beginning with the architects Auguste and Claude Perret. [5] Under the influence of Henry Van de Velde,[6] they had made a very sober facade, but crowned by a splendid fresco by Antoine Bourdelle, representing Apollo and the muses. Then, the three superimposed halls were all decorated by great artists: the frescos by Bourdelle, the ceiling by Maurice Denis, the paintings by Vuillard, the curtain by K.X. Roussel.

Endowed with admirable acoustics, the great hall was naturally dedicated to music and dance. Serge de Diaghilev's Ballets Russes, Pavlova, [7] Chaliapine, [8] Toscanini [9] and so many others have forever marked the history of the theatre.

People were waiting for the chance to trip up Maratier. So he prepared in minute detail his opening production, the première of which took place on April 1 1943. It was *Le Survivant* (The Survivor), a historical play by Jean-François Noël, the subject of which evoked the life of Charles the Bold, Duke of Burgundy. I remember it as though it was yesterday. The staging had been entrusted to Raymond Rouleau, [10] with himself and Serge Reggiani [11] in the principal roles, and Michèle Alfa and Suzanne Flon [12] in the important feminine roles. It was a triumph!

---

5. Theoreticians and practitioners of an architectural neoclassicism based on new materials including concrete, they were called upon as entrepreneurs to construct the Théâtre des Champs-Élysées and took over the project elaborated at the outset by Henry Van de Velde. The building was put up in 1913, based on a framework of reinforced concrete, visible in the pillars of the hall. (EdN)

6. A Belgian architect and decorator, founder with Victor Horta of the Belgian Art Nouveau, a major figure in the modernist movement. (EdN)

7 Anna Pavlova (1881-1931), a Russian ballerina, considered as the greatest classical dancer in the history of ballet. (EdN)

8. Fédor Chaliapine (1873-1938), a Russian opera singer and actor, a legendary bass. (EdN)

9. Arturo Toscanini (1867-1957), legendary Italian conductor, he left Italy to protest against the rise to power of Mussolini and refused to participate in the festivals of Bayreuth and Salzburg to protest against the Nazi racial laws. (EdN)

10. Belgian actor and stage director whose entire career took place in France, his real name being Edgar Rouleau (1904-1981), an outstanding personality in the theatre and cinema, enlisted voluntarily, decorated with the Croix de guerre and the Médaille des engagés volontaires in 1940, having been a prisoner of war. (EdN)

11. Sergio known as Serge Reggiani (1922-2004), a French actor and singer of Italian origin, began his acting career under the occupation, in 1941. (EdN)

12. This role marked the debut of Suzanne Flon in the theatre. (EdN)

The truth of the matter is that Georges Maratier did everything well. Even if, one must admit, the theatre in Paris was generally flourishing under the Occupation: full houses, great actors, beautiful productions.

MAILLOL IN BANYULS

The name "Austerlitz" would sound funny to the ears of someone of German culture: a time of glory for France, of defeat for Austria, the occupation of Vienna by Napoleon's troupes. In 1942, It was Paris' turn to be occupied. And I, a German officer dressed as a civilian, was walking up and down in front of the train that was to take me to the South of France, in the non-occupied part of it. That's how people called it.

We were working with all our might on a big exhibition of Arno Breker's works. Now Breker, who had lived and worked in Paris in 1927, was extremely influenced by the art of Aristide Maillol. Knowing that, I had the idea of going to him and asking him to come up to Paris for the opening of that exhibition. When they accepted my suggestion, my superiors didn't have the slightest notion of the difficulties we would certainly have to overcome. At the beginning of the war, Maillol had withdrawn to Banyuls, his native town, situated of course in the Free Zone. After having presented my proposal in a vague fashion, I explained to my bosses that Maillol would never agree to come. Except if I went specifically to Banyuls and presented my idea to him in person. In fact, I wasn't sure of anything. I confess it. After all, Maillol would perhaps have agreed to come up to Paris without my having to budge. The real reason for my scheme was my dream of crossing the line of demarcation, of going into this non-occupied France. Perhaps I was looking for the pre-war France that I so loved.

Although I was a soldier, I not only had to make this trip as a civilian, but I also needed to obtain an authorization from the Vichy government. Brinon [1] in person was the one who had the papers sent to me *ad hoc*.

It was an express train. Comfortably seated, I looked like a mere civilian off on a holiday in the south. Suddenly, there was no longer either war, or occupation, or anything that could distinguish me from the peaceful French passengers who surrounded me.

To gain time, I had opted for a night train that passed through Orléans. The crossing of the Loire was superb, sparkling. Then, once we approached the line of demarcation, the train stopped at Vierzon: there was an inspection by the German police of identity papers and transit passes. Also, disquiet on the faces of the French passengers. The corporal who inspected our compartment looked at me in a funny way. A German going to "the other side?" He must have found that strange.

Oddly, the stop didn't really last long. I expected more thoroughness, searches and questions. Nothing at all! Everything unfolded as though we were crossing a border in peacetime, or almost. So we set off again quite quickly: Limoges, Cahors, Montauban. Day was beginning to break after Toulouse. There was a very long stop in Narbonne: many people got off, with hundreds of bags and valises. It was no longer a station platform, but a hive. People were running around, and yelling. Then, we went on to Perpignan, Collioure, Port-Vendres and, finally, Banyuls.

The Maillol's home was situated on a height, to the left of the beach. One reached it by means of a pebbly lane that climbed abruptly between old houses.[2] It was a beautiful, hot day. High up, on the right, a wooden door opened up onto a steep staircase with a stone railing, which led to a garden planted with massive trees, and to a pink house with green shutters, the goal of my trip.

The entire Maillol family was gathered in the main room. Everyone was there. Aristide, of course, his wife Clotilde and their son Lucien. Maillol was anxious to go and fetch himself the bottle of Banyuls, and we clinked glasses

---

1. A French lawyer and journalist, Fernand de Brinon published in 1933, in Le Matin, the first interview with Adolf Hitler granted to a French journalist. On becoming a politician, he would, after the defeat of 1940, be a staunch advocate of collaboration. He was the representative of the Vichy Government at the German High Command in Paris during the Occupation, the French ambassador with regard to the Germans, then "the deputy leader of the French Government in the occupied territories." After the denunciation of the armistice treaty and the occupation of the Free Zone in 1942, Fernand de Brinon became the only official representative of the French Government in Paris. He would be shot in Montrouge in 1947. (EdN)

2. Today, this lane is called "Rue A. Maillol." (EdN)

like old friends who had been reunited. It was such a beautiful day that to stay inside would have been a crime. So we set ourselves up outside, on the staircase landing, from which unfolded a magnificent view of the old town of Banyuls, with, as a backdrop, the Albères mountains.

I took advantage of the occasion to carry out an errand for my friend Rudier, who had sold in Paris one of Maillol's large statues and could not managed to get to him the money he was owed. An important sum! The circulation of money was not free between the two zones. I thus had proposed to carry this large package of bills, without really realizing to what I could be exposing myself in the event of a frisking or a systematic search in the train. Currency trafficking was severely punished. No matter! I hadn't given it any thought, that was all. And since things had gone well, I handed the bulky parcel to its consignee. I didn't know what sum I had transported. All I knew was that the package was heavy. Really heavy!

The Banyuls liqueur was stimulating, the conversation got underway easily and very soon there was talk of where I would be lodged. Maillol said that it was impossible to find a room during this season. Banyuls was a fishing village, tourists were rare there and the hotels few in number. Because of the "two Frances" many people had taken up residence there, including mothers with children. The town was overburdened, the Maillols explained to me.

"I have the solution," Aristide said to me. "Dina [3] has gone off on a trip for a while. Her apartment is empty. Lucien will drive you there. Go there right away, then come back, that way, we'll have a nice lunch together."

At noon, the Maillol's home smelled of aromatic herbs. Clotilde was a subtle cook. Her leg of lamb was really excellent.

A large portrait of a woman, a woman of the region, adorned the dining room. I learned that it was the portrait of Lucie, Maillol's aunt. The house where we were had belonged to her, and Aristide had painted this picture a long time ago.

Maillol was not the kind to chat after a meal, nor to take a siesta as is the tradition in the south. Without paying too much attention to the others, he sank into his armchair and started to read. Taking advantage of this respite, because his father had a tendency to monopolize the conversation, Lucien took me out to the garden. He wanted news from Paris. He missed Parisian life. But our tête-à-tête did not last long. With Maillol around, one could not be alone for a

---

3. Dina Vierny, Maillol's model and inspiration. (EdN)

long time. Active by nature and by temperament, he always wanted to organize things, draw people into his orbit. Scarcely had we gone out than Maillol caught up to us carrying a basket filled with figs from the garden.

"Eat, boys," he said to us. "I have gathered them specially for you. After we'll go into the studio."

The studio was in a basement created by the natural slope of the terrain. One accessed it through the garden. Moreover, the entrance was just in front of the big fig tree, whose divine fruits we had just tasted. The room resembled a cellar, the wall of which had been opened up to let in the soft light of the garden, filtered through the foliage. Facing the entrance, a door dug out of the rocky slope led to the wine cellar. "My wife is the one who has the key," Aristide told me with a wink.

Opposite the window stood a large plaster model. "I am working on this statue inspired by Dina," Maillol said, "There are still many things to do on the body itself. The girl still does not have arms. I prefer to work directly on plaster. One can see the details better, and then, one can add or take off more. Look, I have succeeded in placing the left leg by simply moving it forward. And the whole thing remains well balanced. I like it that way, even if the foundry workers don't appreciate my statues being shaped directly in plaster. They consider them too fragile. We have had accidents, it's true. I have found my plaster statues in little pieces from time to time. Now I am very careful."

Without being a chatterbox, Maillol would talk a great deal. But it was always fascinating. For me, at least. To be with him, in his studio, was a real privilege. Because one witnessed incredible things there. Like when he stopped talking suddenly to pick up from the ground a long, sharpened saw. Something on the girl's thigh was visibly bothering him. Consequently, he scraped the spot with the saw, then mixed a bit of plaster and water on a small square piece of wood, to smooth the irregular spot with a spatula, then by hand. It was magic!

Feeling frustrated at being interrupted, once the visit to the studio was over, Lucien took me on a tour of the port, convinced that his father would not follow us. I liked little ports, so I followed him with pleasure. In addition I had never seen the war memorial that Maillol had donated to his native city and which stood, I knew, on a rock, at the spot where the port is united with the sea.

In town, there were really enormous numbers of people, noise, cries, children running everywhere. We found refuge, then, in a bistro next to the beach.

The owner, a friend of Lucien, took all the messages for the Maillols, when there were telephone calls.

It was time for the aperitif. I was not unhappy to find myself in close contact with Lucien, outside of the house, because I needed his advice. Maillol did not yet know that I had come there to persuade him to participate in the opening of Arno Breker's exhibition.

Lucien liked the idea. According to him, "the old man" would be happy to see Paris again, especially his home in Marly-le-Roi, which he had not seen since the beginning of the war. As far as he could tell, it was his mother who might be the problem. I had thought that she obeyed Maillol in everything and, in addition, I believed that women loved Parisian life, especially during the occupation. Well, I got it wrong, apparently. Lucien was sure that it would be necessary to convince his mother first. According to Lucien, if one succeeded in convincing his mother, the problem would be solved.

At that moment, we saw the boats entering the port, full of fresh fish that had just been picked out of the sea. How could one resist such a temptation? So we decided to have dinner there, to move faster. After a night spent in the train, I was quite tired, and was thinking only of my bed, or rather Dina's bed, where I incidentally spent an excellent night.

Well rested, as soon as it was morning I walked over to the pink house. The Maillols had insisted a great deal that we have breakfast together. I entered the kitchen directly, through the green door at the back, where a very pretty table was set. On seeing me, Clotilde exclaimed: "So, I take it, we'll soon see one another in Paris?" Lucien had worked well. There was nothing more I had to do.

Since Aristide did not take breakfast, I found him later in the living room, seated in a large rattan armchair and reading. "My meeting with the Count Harry Kessler [4] was," he told me without beating around the bush, "the greatest stroke of luck in my life. What a man of taste, and what intelligence!"

An extremely wealthy man, who passed away a few years before the start of the war, Harry Kessler had brought together in his very beautiful abode in Weimar, the city of Goethe, an impressive number of masterpieces. Kessler adored France. Sensitive to the most modernist artistic currants of which Paris was

---

4. Art collector, museum director, philanthropist, essay writer, diplomat, active German pacifist, Harry Clemens Ulrich von Kessler died in Lyon in 1937. Harry Kessler was also known for his intimate diary, an essential account of the cosmopolitan and artistic life at the beginning of the 20th century. (EdN)

the capital, he made long and frequent sojourns there. Surrounded by legends and mysteries, the figure of Count Kessler fascinated the high society of Paris. Rumor had it that he was the illegitimate son of the Kaiser, [5] so he was courted. Even more than painting, it was sculpture that fascinated the Count. One often found him at Rodin's. In 1942, I had the immense privilege of meeting Helen von Nostitz, [6] and of hearing her talk about those evenings in Meudon, when she would perform Beethoven sonatas for Rodin and Kessler.

Maillol was too young and too little known to be part of a milieu that was so elitist and so extremely distinguished. But Kessler, who had observed at Vollard's one or two of his terra cotta pieces, was so impressed that he absolutely insisted on showing them to Rodin. He insisted so much that Rodin came over on purpose—an incredible thing—to see them. These first little sculptures by Maillol reminded Kessler so much of Greece that he was absolutely determined to offer the young sculptor a Hellenic voyage of initiation, a voyage to the origins of sculpture. It was a deciding voyage that Maillol had related to me in detail. On arriving in the port of Piraeus, he immediately felt he had come home, because what he saw in that place reminded him of his native Catalonia. Kessler said that the seed sown in antiquity had germinated in Maillol. For him, Maillol created with the same mindset as the Greeks. After Greece, Kessler took him to visit--more than visit, to know--England, then Germany.

When he finished relating all this to me, Maillol took out of the drawer a piece of paper that he handed to me. Paper that he manufactured himself, for his red chalk drawings and woodcuts. The commercial paper that one could buy did not please him. Even the most expensive kind. So he manufacture it himself, using the ancient method, with wire cloths.

"You see this sheet of paper," he asked me? "I sent one like that to Count Kessler in Weimar. And you know what he did? He manufactured them in quantities!"

Kessler, who could offer himself anything he wanted, already had a publishing house. Convinced that this paper thing was an opportunity that was

---

5. A reference to Wilhelm II. (EdN)

6. Née von Benckendorff und Hindenburg, the Countess Helen Lina Olga Vera von Nostitz-Wallwitz (1878-1944) was the descendant of Prince Münster-Ledenburg, a renowned diplomat, and the Russian princess Galitzine, a celebrated music lover. Member of the European cultural elite from a very young age, she was one of the great pianists of her time. Rodin did three portraits of her. Helen von Nostitz inspired Rainer Maria Rilke to write several poems. For Hugo von Hofmannsthal, she was "the most gracious and beautiful young woman" in Europe.

coming his way, he installed a factory not far from Marly, in Montval. A factory intended to produce Maillol's famous artisanal paper. And since it was necessary that things remain in the family, it was Maillol's nephew, Gaspard, who was put in charge of production. The Montval paper mills were born. The very precious paper they produced was used for the rarest and most expensive editions, like the superb volume of Virgil's *Egloges*,[7] illustrated by Maillol's woodcuts.

Clothide entered and interrupted these delicious ramblings with a good bottle of Banyuls. Lunchtime was approaching. Noticing that we were talking about Montval, she exclaimed: "Ah! Again this story of crazies that still enervates me today." And she related to me the following incredible episode.

Count Kessler, who frequented the diplomatic milieus and the high spheres of German power, knew that war between France and Germany was going to occur. [8] Knowing that, it seemed to him normal to inform his friend Maillol about it. Consequently, without nevertheless revealing any state secret, he sent him a telegram in Marly. A lapidary telegram, composed of only three words: "Bury your statues."

Thus Maillol buried several of them in the garden. Not understanding very well what was going on, the neighbours had found this bizarre. For those who knew Kessler, Maillol was "the friend of the Krauts who buried machine guns in his garden and hid military plans in his plaster statues." As for the Montval paper mill that was housed in a barn converted into a factory, at the bottom of a valley, it was in their eyes "the base for bombarding Paris." Thus the mob set fire to the paper mill that was burned from top to bottom. Armed soldiers patrolled in Marly, Maillol risked being arrested at any moment, indeed, killed in a surge of rage. The crowd, the police and the soldiers had invaded his home. The good people were looking for the military plans in the abundant correspondence between Maillol and Kessler. Except that it concerned edition plans, about which "these good people" understood nothing. In short, things could have gone very far, if Clemenceau in person had not intervened, to put an end to this generalized psychosis. It was, alas, too late for the factory. The Montval paper mill was nothing but a pile of ashes. That was the end. Never again would the famous paper be fabricated.

---

7. Also called the Bucolics, the Eglogues are short dialogues between shepherds, with at times some political allusions. In the fourth eglogue, Virgil, for example, exalts the new Golden Age which, for him, was the reign of the Emperor Augustus. (EdN)

8. This reference is to the First World war. (EdN)

"Come and eat," Clotilde said heartily. "I have a roast, not a machine gun, in the oven."

The following afternoon, Maillol accompanied me to the station, On the quay, he handed me a bag filled with grapes, and a freshly baked loaf of bread, saying: "With this, you won't die of hunger." It was truly very touching. At heart, he had remained a peasant.

I didn't have the heart to leave the south of France so quickly. I was in the Free Zone, I had to take advantage of it. So I got off the train at Narbonne. It was a spontaneous decision. It was necessary for me to see the region, to change trains. When I arrived at Marseille late in the evening, I took a room in a very simple hotel, just opposite the Saint-Charles station.

Up at dawn, I spent the day being a tourist with a determination that I didn't think I possessed. Completely exhausted at the end of the day, I sat down at a table on a sidewalk terrace, at Basso's, a restaurant on the Quai des Belges. While waiting for my bouillabaisse, I ordered an aperitif. Scarcely did I have time to take a sip of it than a man asked me politely whether he could join me. His German was tinged with a strong Berlin accent. A bit surprised at first to be recognized, indeed, spotted so easily and in such an indisputable way, I quickly forgot my surprise, because the man was voluble, visibly happy to be speaking in his maternal tongue. And to empty his heart, a heart filled with misery. He was a well known businessman in Berlin. A Jewish businessman. By a stroke of luck, he succeeded in leaving Germany at the very beginning of the war, and living since then in France. First in Paris, then in the Free Zone. Disoriented, unable to really comprehend what had happened to him, nor to make ends meet, he was nostalgic, lost and confused. He was asking me for advice, me, a stranger. I was very embarrassed. Also touched, of course. Obviously, I could not tell him that I was an officer in the Wehrmacht. Given what he had already told me, the poor man would have been terrified. I told him, then, that I was somewhat in the same situation as he was, not for racial reasons, but because of my political opinions. He believed me or pretended to believe me. I offered him a bouillabaisse that he accepted with joy, and we spent an excellent evening sharing our memories of Berlin before 1933. He was the first and last German Jewish refugee I would meet during the whole war.

The next morning, I took the train for Nice. A magnificent ride along the coast. There, I settled into the Hôtel Royal, [9] in a very beautiful room, with a

9. A three star hotel today. (EdN)

big balcony overlooking the Promenade des Anglais. I had only to cross it to go swimming.

As everyone knows, the Promenade des Anglais is followed by the Promenade des États-Unis, where, to my surprise, I saw American soldiers standing guard in front of their Consulate General. Being in Nice, I couldn't refrain from going over to the Casino, next to the Palais de la Méditerranée. To enter, I got myself a stamped "carte de légitimation" (legitimization card), in my name.

I kept it on me during the whole duration of the war.

Three years later, I found myself for my misfortune in Berlin, surrounded, closed in by the Russians. As a refugee in a peripheral area in the south of the capital, I had traded my officer's uniform for a priest's cassock. My military papers, my identity papers had all been burned. The only thing I had left was this card from the Casino in Nice.

Since the defeat of Germany was consummated, what had to happen happened: one day I was arrested by a Russian patrol. A silly routine check. The under-officer, I don't know what rank he held, a sergeant, perhaps a caporal, was questioning me more or less, in more than broken German. I handed him the card from the Casino in Nice, the only "identity paper" I had left, while telling him that I had been brought to Germany as a French worker, and that I was trying to return to my home town of Nice. I was speaking very slowly, trying to make mistakes in my German. And it worked. After listening to me carefully, the Russian offered me a cigarette, and said: "Safe return to France."

I had escaped by the skin of my teeth. If he had discovered that I was really an active officer in disguise, and thus a fraudster, he would have taken me prisoner, and I would have ended up in a camp in the depths of Russia. So the Nice Casino card had saved my life.

On my return to Paris, I saddled Maillol with the responsibility for my long absence, saying that he was "difficult to convince," "impossible to persuade," etc. Even though Aristide and Clotilde had accepted right away, their only fear being the crossing from the Free zone into the Occupied Zone. They feared the difficulties, the hassles, whereas it was in fact very simple. By agreeing to come to Paris, Maillol had accompanied his agreement with a condition: "Come pick us up in person, with all the papers, so that we don't have to take care of it." Obviously, I accepted with joy.

In the meantime, the preparations for the Breker exhibition were moving full steam ahead. Everything was going well, but new problems cropped up every day. I was, if I may say so, on the firing line. I really couldn't absent myself for several days, just to go fetch the Maillols at the other end of France. I informed my direct superior, Lieutenant Lucht, about it, and another member of the *Propagandastaffel* was designated to perform this very agreeable task, I must say.

The day they arrived in the capital, I went over to welcome them, at the Austerlitz station, in the company of Mimina Breker. [10] The *Propagandastaffel* had reserved them a lovely apartment on the first floor of the Claridge. With, from the balcony, a magnificent view of the Champs-Élysées. Everybody paid court to such a celebrated couple. The French, of course, but especially the Germans. The receptions in their honour followed one another, including the one offered by Otto Abetz at the Hôtel Beauharnais.

Nevertheless, on the day of the inauguration, [11] Aristide asked me to stay a bit in the background. He did not wish to advance up to the rank of honour, and be placed among the "official representatives" where he was nevertheless expected. Thus he would hear from afar the inaugural speech by Abel Bonnard. [12] Nor did one see him next to Arno and Mimina Breker, Brinon, Benoist-Méchin, [13] General Barkhausen, Otto Abetz, Serge Lifar, Jean Cocteau and so many other celebrities who had come to take part in the event.

Maillol was unhappy at the Claridge: too many visits, too many solicitations. He absolutely wanted to go home. It was impossible to hold him back. He had come, as promised, now he desired ardently to return to his dwelling, in Banyuls. This time, I accompanied him and Clotilde up to the line of demarcation. We said farewell to one another in Vierzon.

---

10. The wife of the sculptor Arno Breker, a former Rodin model. (EdN)

11. Inaugurated on May 15, the Arno Breker exhibition closed on July 31 1942. (EdN)

12. A fascist intellectual, member of the Académie française, Minister of National Education and of Youth in the Vichy Government, a diehard collaborationist, a self-confessed homosexual nicknamed "Gestapette" by the underground resistance, Abel Bonnard would be condemned to death in absentia in 1945. Having taken refuge in Madrid, he would die there in 1968. (EdN)

13. A French intellectual and politician, Jacques Michel Gabriel Paul Benoist-Méchin, (1901-1983), was condemned to death in 1947, then pardoned. (EdN)

ARNO BREKER IN BANYULS
OCTOBER 1943

A portrait painter of great talent, Breker took it into his head to do the bust of Maillol. Since he couldn't ask the latter to pose in Paris and, even less, in Germany, there remained for him only one possibility: to go down to Banyuls.

We were in 1943. There was no longer any "Free Zone." Breker, who had carefully prepared his visit to Maillol, planned on travelling to Catalonia by car. And... he asked me to accompany him. At that time, no one refused Breker anything. So I took the train to Mulhouse, where we were to meet.

Their car was fully loaded. Notably, with a crate that held Maillol's portrait sketched from photos.

Belfort, Besançon, Arbois, Lons-le-Saunier, the crossing of the Rhône near Saint-Genix-en-Savoie, then Grenoble, our first stop. The first, because René d'Uckermann, who had taken charge of Arno Breker's book on sculpture, published by Flammarion on the occasion of his Parisian exhibition, had invited the Brekers to spend a few days in his domain of La Tronche, [1] very near Grenoble.

The beautiful estate had formerly belonged to the painter Hébert. [2] It was composed of two buildings, connected by a gallery, on the roof of which a terrace offered a splendid view of the Alps. The interior was filled with Hébert's paintings and precious art objects. Uckermann was accustomed to spend the summer in this residence. I knew it, because I had obtained passes for him more than once, when that region was still in the Free Zone. When we ar-

---

1. René Patris-d'Uckermann, a member of the Académie Delphinale, literary director of the éditions Flammarion, friend of Jules Romains, François Mauriac, Louise Weiss, Maurice Genevoix, and Roger Peyrefitte, who all sojourned at La Tronche. (EdN)

2 . Ernest Hébert (1817-1908), a French painter, who died at La Tronche. (EdN)

rived, we were not only greeted by René d'Uckermann, but also by Claude, the young son of Henri Flammarion. As a notability of the region, our host had invited the prefect and his assistant to lunch. After the meal, sitting on the terrace, amidst the orange trees, we suddenly heard a strong explosion. Embarrassed, the prefect told us: "They are blowing up military material." The "they" meant naturally "the Résistance." The countryside was swarming with underground fighters. I had told that to the Brekers.

Being in the region, we could not neglect visiting the Grande Chartreuse. The visit was too rapid, alas, but we had to pursue our route. To shorten it, we took the risk of driving over the isolated passage through the Alps, by way of the Napoleon road, until Gap. Arno Breker determined the itinerary according to the things he wanted to see and the places he wanted to visit. After Gap, it was Nyons, Orange, Avignon, Nîmes, Montpellier, Béziers, Perpignan and Port-Vendres. Having advised the Brekers about the difficulties of finding lodgings in Banyuls, especially for several people, we set ourselves up in Port-Vendres, a few minutes by car from the Maillols.

The next day, once we had eaten breakfast, we hastened to go to Banyuls. Our arrival at the pink house touched off an explosion of joy for everybody. Scarcely had we made ourselves comfortable, scarcely had the conversation begun, than Maillol was already drawing Breker to the basement, into his studio where stood the unfinished plaster form of *l'Harmonie*. I helped Breker transport his crate with the started bust, so that he could begin work when the time came. The posing sessions started as of the following morning. Maillol would stand in front of the window in his studio, and Breker would begin working. It was out of the question to disturb them. I did so however one day, at the request of Clotilde, who said to me in a tone that would not suffer contradiction: "Go fetch the men, it is time to sit down at the table." An excellent cook and a person of exquisite hospitality, Mme Maillol had insisted that all the meals be taken at her place. And indeed, for the whole duration of the work. So I went down into the cave of creation to call "the men" to the table, and I made use of this to take several photos which are the only documents confirming that these special sessions between Maillol and Breker really occurred. Having really nothing to do during such extended periods, we availed ourselves of the car. One day, we went to Spain, another time, Mimina, Lucien and I paid a visit to Raoul Dufy who had been in Perpignagn since the beginning of the war. He was living in a ground floor apartment, on the rue de la Gare. Not very large, with a little room arranged as a studio. Dufy had returned from a stay in the country, near Toulouse, with a big portfolio full of pastoral sketches.

When the bust was finished, Breker called Rudier who sent his caster, Renucci, right away to Banyuls, to make the plaster molding on the spot. As for Breker, he didn't talk about it, but Maillol was very happy with the result.

We were getting ready to set out for the return trip, when, to our great surprise, Maillol asked Breker to take him along too. Using as a pretext the possibility that his caster would put on sale without his agreement the heads of the T*rois Grâces*, he said he was anxious to bring "all that" into the open. In reality, as I would find out later, he was worried about the fate of his model, Dina, from whom he had not had any news for a long time. Breker hesitated at first, because of Maillol's advanced age, but there was nothing he could do. Since Maillol insisted a great deal, we were "one more" on our departure day.

First stop, Cahors. An important place for the Résistance. We had to be careful. Because we could easily find ourselves with a bomb under the car. The chauffeur was strictly forbidden from opening his mouth. He didn't know a word of French. The large dining room of the hotel was filled with people who all looked like underground fighters. They were underground fighters, I was sure of it. So we had dinner quickly, and our conversation was of the most sober variety. The next stop, Blois. Then, Paris, where we arrived safe and sound.

The Brekers checked in at the Ritz where they were habitués. As for myself, I took Maillol with me to the Lincoln, my accustomed domicile, because I wanted us to stay together. Every morning, I would prepare some good coffee, I would buy croissants across the street, and we would have breakfast together. Maillol would relate to me his feminine adventures, numerous but short-lived. He also talked to me about the ferocious jealousy of his wife who even managed to drive his models away.

This time, he enjoyed being in Paris. Once Dina came back, he said, he would finish the *Harmonie*, would put his works in order, and sort out the real and fake prints. Because while we were taking our breakfasts at the Lincoln, Dina was arrested. Obviously, we were not aware of it.

But Dina was not Maillol's only cause for worry. Quite a while before then he had commissioned Rudier to cast the *Trois Grâces*, a work done between 1936 and 1938, if my memory serves me right. The three nudes had been cast separately, and the pedestal as well. The pieces now had to be brought together, chiselled and polished up. Maillol was very anxious to be present at this phase of the work. Thus Rudier came by to call on him at the hotel on day "J", and all three of us went by car to the foundry.

Maillol did not want the lead castings to be covered with any patina. He wanted light to be reflected in the metal. This required a particular kind of work, because it would be necessary to make the cuts, joints, etc., disappear.

When we got to Malakoff, the *Trois Grâces* were already at the back of the courtyard. The light was well reflected, and no flaw, no joint, no soldering was perceptible. Visibly satisfied, Maillol walked around the sculpture, ran his hand over the lead buttocks of the Graces, sometimes indicated to Rudier the final hammering to be done, while repeating, "Now that is a beautiful shape, a very beautiful shape. And the girls remain standing, without breaking. If you knew how much I have worried about them!"

Obviously, we were curious to know the story.

As was his custom, whenever it was a question of creating large-scale works, Maillol would mould them first in plaster. And then one morning, he would find the figure in the middle lying on the ground, in pieces in the middle of the studio. The first accident. Without getting discouraged, he resumed his work and the young girl stood up again; only her arms were missing. To verify the exactness of the casting, Maillol had the habit of running his hand over the model's contours, then over the plaster version. And just when he was in the process of caressing the body of the young lady who posed for him, the door opened abruptly. It was Clothilde. A huge scandal! So huge that the model had to leave right away, without further ado. This was why the third Grace remained without arms. Very vexed, Maillol executed the arms from memory, but in the end was never satisfied with the result. Frankly, once the three Graces were reassembled, one could not find anything at all amiss. Nevertheless, Maillol would not budge an inch. For him, the arms of the Grace in the middle were badly done. And when Rudier asked him for permission to set up that very girl in the middle in the park surrounding his home in Le Vésinet, Maillol agreed, but on the express condition that the arms be cut. I had always admired this sculpture at Rudier's place. Maillol was right, it was better without the "false arms."

DINA VIERNY

When I first sojourned in Banyuls, I took advantage of Dina's apartment during her absence. But I met her later, in Paris, when she came to visit me at 52 avenue des Champs-Élysées to convey to me the master's best regards.

From then on, we had gone out together quite a lot; to Korniloff's, the former head chef of Nicolas II; at the Robinson, run by my friends the Blandeaus.

But she had gone off again quite quickly, because Maillol needed her to finish the *Harmonie*. Since then, I had not heard from her.

But one day, on my return from my second stay in Banyuls, the one where I accompanied the Brekers, I found in my office a strange envelope, mailed from Belfort. The paper was cut out in a circle, covered by a very small handwriting and jam stains. Intrigued, then stupefied, I read the following: "Werner, I am imprisoned in Fresnes. Come quickly and save me. Dina." The address of my particular service was, it too, written in a circle. After reading and re-reading the missive, I heaved a sigh of relief. Not because she was arrested, but because her extravagant and illegal letter had, by some miracle, slipped through the net of the military censorship that monitored us as well.

Dina was of Russian origin, but Jewish. Her real name was Orloff. I knew that. This was not good. Not good at all, because the Fresnes prison depended on the Gestapo. In fact, it could not have been worse. She could be deported at any moment, if she wasn't already.

With a naive air, I went fishing for information on rue des Saussaies, and found out that Dina had been arrested for trafficking in dollars. I thought that this in itself was not so grave. But I was mistaken. I began then taking the necessary steps for her release, when I was suddenly summoned by Lieutenant

Lucht, who showed me a letter signed by Himmler himself, the contents of which said in substance that "this Russian Jew" had to be liquidated. How could I obtain a release after reading "that"? With a sang-froid that still astonishes me, I said to Lucht, looking at him straight in the face, "Herr Lucht, I have never read this letter, and I have never heard about its contents." Lucht lowered his head and did not answer anything.

The guards and the little SS people who were in charge of Dina could not have been informed about all that. But on the other hand, I could not be sure that Lucht would keep the secret. So it was necessary to act fast. On phoning the rue des Saussaies a second time, I found out that Dina was precisely "within the walls", and facing an interrogation. Knowing their methods and their techniques, I asked the guy not to treat her too roughly, and told him that she was not really sharp, that she had not set the world on fire. This, of course, was not true. On the contrary, Dina was very intelligent. Visibly amused, my interlocutor told me suddenly that if I wanted to see her, all I had to do was come to his office. I couldn't believe my ears. It was about noon. "To go and see her," meant "getting her out." I asked my secretary to phone immediately the Rudiers, the Brekers, Lucht, and above all Maillol, who was still at the Hôtel Lincoln, and invite them for lunch on avenue Matignon, at the Grand restaurant near the Hôtel Berkeley.

When I reached the rue des Saussaies, I ran up the steps of the staircase four by four. They led to the office indicated, and I came face to face with Dina, seated nicely on a chair, the very picture of innocence.

"You can take this girl with you, Herr Lange," someone said to me. "We are closing for lunch. Tomorrow, you will go with her to Fresnes and pick up her belongings!"

I gave the formal salute, and we walked towards the exit, without further ado. Chattering enough for two people, Dina was already starting to talk to me in the corridors. "Shut up!" I muttered between my teeth. Once in the street, we could talk to one another at last. I thought that after Fresnes, she surely wanted a good lunch. So we walked toward avenue Matignon, where our friends were assembled. And who, moreover, were probably wondering why I was late.

When we entered the restaurant, I opened the door with a theatrical gesture and pushed Dina inside. Everyone was very moved, especially old Maillol. Surprised to see his preferred model from whom he had not had any news for so long, the poor man had become completely pale. Dina, however, like a good actress, and playing the principal role as well, did not look upset in the least.

Quietly, as though nothing had happened, she picked up the menu to order her meal. Then ate with the greatest satisfaction.

The next day, I had to go to Fresnes with her. I could not avoid it. Under the stares of all these SS, the visit was quite embarrassing.

A woman from Belfort had shared her cell. Fifteen years later, I saw her again in Paris, on the street. She recognized me.

I was afraid that once she was free, Dina would start causing trouble again. In Paris there were many temptations. I thus succeeded in convincing her to return to Banyuls without delay. To make really sure that she did, I accompanied her personally to the station.

To thank me no doubt, Maillol brought me a beautiful red chalk drawing of a woman reclining, seen from behind. It was a former model, before Dina's time. There was a dedication: "To my friend Lange."

Now that Dina had gone back, he wanted to leave too. I accompanied him, then, again till Vierson. There we bid each other farewell, not knowing that this would be a real farewell, a definitive farewell. In the spring of 1944, I received the dreadful news of his death: a car accident. He was returning from Perpignan with his friend, a doctor, after having visited Dufy.

When he heard the news, Otto Abetz said that Maillol was probably killed by the Résistance, because of his good relations with the Germans. Never did I believe that version. I felt that to use Maillol's name for counter-propaganda purposes was the epitome of bad taste.

ARNO BREKER

Like numerous European artists, Arno Breker had, in his youth, lived and worked in Paris. In Montparnasse, to be more precise. Influenced by Maillol, he produced at that time very fine statuettes, the size of which was determined by the very modest dimensions of his studio. After Paris, he treated himself to an important and formative stay in Rome, before settling definitively in Berlin with Mimina, a young Greek woman whom he had married in the interval. Breker excelled particularly in the portrait, his preferred genre, thanks notably to the extreme subtlety of his art. But he dreamed of great works, of monumental ones, which explains why he realized his famous Prometheus. This great nude male statue gave so much pleasure to the new regime established in Germany in 1933, that it bought the sculpture and commissioned others right away, destined to adorn the new chancellery of the Third Reich, which Albert Speer was to build, and which he built by the way: an immense pile erected on Voss street, in which everything was too big. And whose disproportionate neo-classical style had something inept about it. The hall of mirrors there was far bigger in size than the one at Versailles. As for Hitler's office, it had, quite simply, unreal dimensions. To adorn the main portal, Speer ordered two statues from Breker, that were, they, too, of unreal size, and also an unusual quantity of bas-reliefs for the inside. The two colossal nudes, *The Torch Bearer*, and *The Sword Bearer*, [1] marked the beginning of Arno Breker's official career. Thanks to the sizeable budget that Albert Speer was managing, Breker was able to realize very highly crafted, very smooth statues, of a virile and heroic nature if they were to be men, and full of grace if they were

---

1. These statues stood on either side of the entrance to the new chancellery in Berlin, but were destroyed during the war. (EdN)

to be women. I admit that I appreciated his work that I had known since the 1930s. Admittedly, most critics praised the grandeur without grandiloquence of his talent. The extraordinary way he had of arranging the hair of his women earned him the title of "the best hairdresser in Berlin."

Breker knew Paris so well that he was the one who had served as Hitler's guide during the latter's brief visit in 1940. He liked Paris and came there often. That is how I got to know him.

Breker had always dreamed of a Parisian exhibition. Hence his "historical" exhibition at the Orangerie in the Tuileries Gardens that no one, I can bear witness to this, envisaged as such. He had chosen that hall from among so many others, because he could exhibit there his large-scale sculptures. When he became Minister of Armaments, Speer was so enthusiastic about the project that he committed himself to providing the metals necessary for the casting of these works. It was enormous!

The plaster moldings were shipped to Rudier, because he was the one who would cast the pieces. As for the designs, they landed in my office and I had to take charge of having them framed.

At the outset, The Arts Services in Berlin had received the order to take charge of the exhibition from A to Z. Except that I discovered rapidly that nothing would be done, and that the exhibition would not take place, at least not on the designated dates, if I didn't assume the responsibility for it personally. I confess that I was the one who had suggested the Orangerie to Breker. Not only because of its location in the centre of Paris, but because important artistic manifestations had been organized there. Breker had immediately deemed the idea excellent. The Orangerie, however, depended on the National Museum of the Louvre, an institution that we all resepcted. So I went to see Monsieur Jaujard,[2] its director, to explain the project to him.

His office was on the ground floor, in the wing situated between the Mollien Pavilion and the Great Gallery on the quay, and one entered it from the Place du Carrousel. I had visited Jacques Jaujard so often that I could find my way

---

2. Appointed director of the national museums and the School of the Louvre in 1940, Jacques Jaujard (1895-1967) organized during the war, and against the orders of the Vichy Government, the evacuation of the artworks of the Museum of the Louvre to the south of France. He was also instrumental in saving important private collections, including the one owned by Maurice de Rotchschild. Appointed as General Manager of Fine Arts at the Liberation, he was decorated with the Medal of the Resistance and named Commander, then Great Cross of the Legion of Honour. (EdN)

there easily. His secretary, Mme Saupique, the wife of the sculptor, [3] always received me very amiably. I very much enjoyed speaking with Monsieur Jaujard, an older colleague and an eminent connoisseur of the arts. He had great admiration for Wilhelm von Bode [4] whom I also admired enormously, because more than anyone else, he was instrumental in giving the museums of Berlin their world reputation. He knew that before becoming an officer, I was a fine arts professional and had worked on great collections. Consequently we often talked about the need to protect artworks in these dreadful times of war. Thus, I was entirely in the know about the Louvre's preparations, then of the evacuation of artworks to the provinces. I had even viewed and leafed through the documents listing the works ready to be sent off.

Half out of curiosity and half jokingly I had asked him where la Joconde was. Without hesitating, he replied that she was in the Ingres Museum in Montauban, with numerous other pictures as well. Then he explained to me that this deposit in Montauban was causing him considerable anxiety, because atmospheric conditions there were very different from the ones in Paris, and he feared that the colours might be damaged or altered. It was absolutely necessary to find touch-up varnish, which, alas, was impossible to find because of the war. Even Count von Metternich to whom he had appealed when explaining the problem to him, was unable to offer help. Whereas I, through a combination of circumstances, was able to come to the rescue thanks to the Lefebvre-Foinet establishment [5] that supplied me in my capacity as an amateur painter. I knew that Maurice hid all kinds of things in the cellar. It was impossible for him not to have a can or two of touch-up varnish. He could not refuse my request and I passed them on to Jacques Jaujard.

Thus, when I presented my Breker project to him for the Orangerie, he gave me his consent unhesitatingly. Besides, he appreciated Breker's talent, outside of any political implications. That went without saying.

So things had started moving very well, except that it was necessary to work on the printing of the catalogue without delay. To wait for the Arts Service in Berlin to do this would be the equivalent of suicide. It was absolutely

---

3. Georges Saupique (1889-1961), a French sculptor. Several of his works are displayed at the Louvre and in the Rodin Museum in Meudon. (EdN)

4. Former director of the museums in Berlin. (EdN)

5. A famous painting establishment that is no longer in existence today, located in Montparnasse at the corner of the rue Vavin and the rue Bréa.(EdN)

necessary to edit and print it in Paris. When Henri Flammarion offered his services spontaneously, the artistic and editorial management of the project was entrusted to René d'Uckermann. He resided at the Hôtel Montmoren- cy-Bours,[6] on the rue du Cherche-Midi, a gift of Napoléon to "Madame Sans- Gêne." This magnificent property was endowed with a beautiful stairway, and the hôtel's decoration testified to M. d'Uckermann's exquisite taste.

As one could have expected, the result was irreproachable: a catalogue of 120 pages enhanced by 120 engravings and a superb text bearing the signature of Charles Despiau. The poor man would suffer for this text after the Libera- tion, whereas it is very probable that he did not write it, but simply signed it.

Everything was going smoothly, when suddenly the Gestapo "discovered" that Mme Flammarion née Engel, Angel in German, was Jewish. How did they know this? In fact, they knew nothing, but for them she must have been Jewish since her maiden name was, in their eyes, typically "Jewish." I knew the Flammarions well. They were all practising Lutherans. I didn't know what to asnwer. I was terrified. If the Gestapo's suspicions were confirmed, the edi- tion would be threatened and we would not have any catalogue.

When he got wind of the news, Arno Breker, beside himself with rage, ran to see the head of the Gestapo who, naturally, had heard of Hitler's uncon- ditional admiration for the artist. The "Madame Engel wife of Flammarion" affair was thus buried right then and there.

Everything was going well, I was happy. Except that on the day of the opening of the exhibition, I realized that no one in Berlin had thought about printing tickets or entrance vouchers! Once again, I had to appeal to M. Jaujard who kindly came to our rescue with several rolls of tickets from the Louvre.

The day of the opening, truly very solemn, more because of the presence of the French than the Germans, I listened, lost in the crowd, and standing next to the Maillols and the Rudiers, to the speeches of Bonnard and Benoist-Méchin. Vlaminck, Derain, Friesz, and van Dongen had refrained from coming.

The guests at the opening were treated to a magnificent concert by the pinaists Wilhelm Kempff and Alfred Cortot, and also by the singer Germaine Lubin.

The large bronzes exhibited in Paris were all intended to adorn the squares and avenues of Berlin. It was said that Speer was just waiting for the end of

---

6. Located at 85 rue du Cherche-Midi, also called the Petit Hôtel de Montmorency, bought in 1752 by Count de Montmorency-Bours, it is now the Musée Hébert, an annex of the Musée d'Orsay. (EdN)

the war to launch his immense plans to transform the capital of the Reich. We know what followed.

Be that as it may, and in all honesty, even in these large statues, Arno Breker had succeeded in safeguarding the sensibility he showed at the beginning of his career. The faces of these colossuses were real portraits. I had seen him work in Banyuls on Maillol's bust. And later on, on Vlaminck's. Breker almost managed to make his sculptures come alive. One needs only take a look at his portrait of Jean Cocteau as well.

THE END

According to what they were telling us, the German generals did not fear the Allied landing very much. They were expecting it and were prepared for it. The only uncertainty, the only anxiety, then, was the place.

So we were not suprised on June 6 1944, on learning the news. On the other hand, the thrust from Avranches unleashed general consternation. The Allied forces had blasted through our defense and could now pour over the whole of France. Overcome by panic, the German civilians were now leaving Paris where their lives had been so agreeable. Followed quite rapidly, I must say, by different military services.

At the beginning of August, I received the order to show up at the Eastern Fort, in Saint-Denis. The Kommandantur had made the decision to defend Paris instead of declaring it an "open city," as I had hoped. Since I had to show up there in uniform, without anything else, I left my personal effects at the Hôtel Lincoln, whose owner not only had an English appearance but also cross-channel ideas, if I may say so. I knew this, because she had always spoken quite freely with me. There again, she shook my hand warmly, and said: "Good luck!" She didn't like either the Occupation or the occupier, but we liked each other a lot, despite everything.

The Eastern Fort was part of the former fortifications of Paris. I should add that it had lost its military character and was not located in Saint-Denis itself. It was a large rectangular courtyard, lined with old edifices and surrounded by vague ramparts. The commandant of the fort, an old captain, was more than old enough for retirement. Moreover he did not have all that many people to command. Some soldiers, very few in number, were loitering around and chatting. The whole set up looked frankly laughable. On seeing me arrive, the captain told me that there had to be a canon somewhere in the buildings. He didn't know where. But since I was formally attached to the artillery, he ordered me to find it and to set up the defense of the fort around it.

I quickly discovered the canon. It was in a shed. An old thing, already too old, no doubt, even in 1914-18. It should have been placed in front of the Invalides, next to other antiques. That was my opinion. But a soldier does not exist to think. He is there to carry out orders. Better: to obey! With the help of several soldiers, we managed to roll out the antique to the middle of the courtyard, facing the entrance. Now it was necessary to find ammunition. As for ammunition, there was none. All we could do was hope that the mere sight of this terrible war machine would impress the enemy to the point of making it flee.

The days unfolded peacefully. It was hot and we often went swimming. There were always French people on the bridge, in front of the entrance to the fort, curious to see what was going on inside. We did not chase them away. Everything was calm. All seemed to function well. Even the telephone, that allowed me to stay in contact with my Parisian friends. Especially with the Rudiers, with whom I had become close. But one fine day, the telephone was silenced. It no longer worked. No one was informing us anymore about anything. To such an extent that the French, gathered on the bridge, had become our one and only source of information. They were the ones to tell us that the Leclerc Division was at the gates of Paris. And that the first manifestations of the Resistance had occurred in the capital. Thus one day one of the gaping onlookers handed me a copy of the newspaper called "Free France." I had never seen one of them before. In one, there was an ironic account of the forced flight of the Vichy Government to Baden-Baden, then to Sigmaringen. I remember the title: "From one spa town to another spa town."

From time to time, soldiers came up to tell me that "things" were happening outside of our puny fortifications. We were enclosed, isolated, and the poor devils were wondering what would become of them. I told them that if we were taken prisoners, we would probably not budge from here. The fort was a perfect detention place. They didn't find that very funny.

One day, a lovely surprise, I saw Rudier arrive. Not having any news from me, since the telephone was cut off, he came to make sure that I was well. And when he noticed that I didn't have much to do, he proposed to take me over to Le Vésinet where a good meal was waiting for us. I accepted with joy, as much for the meal as for the opportunity to have news. We were really cut off from the world.

When the meal was over, as delicious as it always was at their home, the Rudiers advised me with one voice to desert, and not return to the fort. They were ready to put me up and hide me until the Germans left. That would not be long in coming, given the state of things. They were right, I knew it. But that was a decision with heavy consequences. Upset, disoriented, I returned to my office on the Champs-Élysées, from which everybody had fled. There was no longer anything or anyone.

I spent the night in the corridor, without closing an eye, stretched out on a sofa that was uncomfortable and too short. In the morning, I made my decision. I could not desert. If I were declared a deserter, my mother would have suffered the consequences: terrible persecution at the hands of the Nazi regime. That was the rule. I had to return to the fort.

The next morning, I left 52 avenue des Champs-Élysées definitively, and returned to my fort. Two days of unjustified absence was no small matter in time of war. I apprehended the interview with the captain. But, finally, everything went rather well. After a severe but brief bawling out, he told me that only the circumstances had prevented him from sending a report to "you know where." There was no need to be more precise, I had understood. I didn't know whether I should thank him or not. With a weary gesture, he dismissed me. And I went to sleep near the old canon.

The weather continued being lovely. All was calm, on the surface. Even if outside, one could see a strange ballet of cars, a ceaseless coming and going. At night, there was some light in the stairwell of the large building, opposite the fort. One could see men going up and down briskly. I don't know why, but I was convinced that there were secret meetings of the Résistance or of the underground as it was called then.

On Thursday August 24, all the bells of Paris began to ring. One could hear nothing but that. Almost opposite us, I could hear the bells of the Sacré-Coeur and, further away, those of Notre-Dame. It was the liberation of Paris. We had understood this without our being told.

We were waiting for orders. Anything! But nothing came. Neither the next day nor the days afterward. One would have thought that our little garrison had been abandoned. That is what we were thinking, in any case. And since no one was attacking us, we didn't budge. It was dead quiet. Until that evening when a truck approached the entrance to the fort: a truck full of German soldiers and things, all mixed up in a heartbreaking disorder. With one jump, I was in it.

This is how my career as an occupier ended, without glory, I must say. On leaving Paris in this very inglorious way, in this truck, I didn't know if I would return there one day. But I did return there, no longer as an occupier, but as a lover: a bashful and grateful lover.

INDEX